FORTRESS • 83

ROMAN AUXILIARY FORTS 27 BC–AD 378

DUNCAN B CAMPBELL

ILLUSTRATED BY BRIAN DELF

Series editors Marcus Cowper and Nikolai Bogdanovic

First published in 2009 by Osprey Publishing
Midland House, West Way, Botley, Oxford OX2 0PH, UK
443 Park Avenue South, New York, NY 10016, USA
E-mail: info@ospreypublishing.com

ISBN 978 1 84603 380 3

Editorial by Ilios Publishing Ltd, Oxford, UK (www.iliospublishing.com)
Page layout by Ken Vail Graphic Design, Cambridge, UK (kvgd.com)
Typeset in Sabon and Myriad Pro
Cartography: Map Studio, Romsey, UK
Index by Alison Worthington
Originated by PDQ Media, Bungay, UK

09 10 11 12 13   10 9 8 7 6 5 4 3 2 1

A CIP catalogue record for this book is available from the British Library.

FOR A CATALOGUE OF ALL BOOKS PUBLISHED BY OSPREY MILITARY AND AVIATION PLEASE CONTACT:

Osprey Direct, c/o Random House Distribution Center, 400 Hahn Road, Westminster, MD 21157
E-mail: uscustomerservice@ospreypublishing.com

Osprey Direct, The Book Service Ltd, Distribution Centre, Colchester Road, Frating Green, Colchester, Essex, CO7 7DW
E-mail: customerservice@ospreypublishing.com

www.ospreypublishing.com

ARTIST'S NOTE

Readers may care to note that the original paintings from which the colour plates in this book were prepared are available for private sale. All reproduction copyright whatsoever is retained by the Publishers. All enquiries should be addressed to:

Brian Delf, 7 Burcot Park, Burcot, Abingdon, OX14 3DH, UK

The Publishers regret that they can enter into no correspondence upon this matter.

THE FORTRESS STUDY GROUP (FSG)

The object of the FSG is to advance the education of the public in the study of all aspects of fortifications and their armaments, especially works constructed to mount or resist artillery. The FSG holds an annual conference in September over a long weekend with visits and evening lectures, an annual tour abroad lasting about eight days, and an annual Members' Day.

The FSG journal *FORT* is published annually, and its newsletter *Casemate* is published three times a year. Membership is international. For further details, please contact:

The Secretary, c/o 6 Lanark Place, London W9 1BS, UK

Website: www.fsgfort.com

THE WOODLAND TRUST

Osprey Publishing are supporting the Woodland Trust, the UK's leading woodland conservation charity, by funding the dedication of trees.

ACKNOWLEDGEMENTS

It is again a pleasure to acknowledge the kindness and generosity of friends and colleagues who provided illustrations for this little book, or who assisted in their supply. Most are acknowledged in the photo captions, but I should like to mention Barbara Berry, who supplied photos of The Lunt Roman Fort; Erik Dobat (http://www.limesfilm.com), who supplied photos of Danubian sites; Mark Hassall, who permitted the adaptation and use of his fort plans; and Mike Bishop, who supplied photo references for the Qasr Bshir plate.

DEDICATION

To Alan Leslie, in whose pleasant company I have rambled over many fort sites.

A NOTE ON THE SOURCES

All ancient sources are referenced using the abbreviations recommended by *The Oxford Classical Dictionary*. All translations are my own.

CONTENTS

ROMAN AUXILIARY FORTS 27 BC–AD 378

INTRODUCTION

The fort at Aquis Querquennis (Galiza, Spain), established under the Flavian emperors. Two granaries and a large courtyard building can be seen in the far corner. (© Antonio Rodriguez Colmenero)

The ancient writers of the classical world used the terms *castra* (in Greek, *stratopedon*) and its diminutive, *castellum* (in Greek, *phrouria*), to designate the permanent fortifications of the Roman Army. When the early scholars of Romano-British archaeology set about codifying their knowledge of Roman military sites, they adopted the term 'fortress' as a translation of *castra*, to represent the great legionary encampments. The smaller *castellum* was rendered as a 'fort', and came to be associated with the auxiliary units of the Roman Army. However, ancient writers frequently employed alternative terms, such as *praesidium*, which simply indicates a guard post or garrison

of some kind, and (as we shall see) archaeology has revealed that Roman fortifications came in various shapes and sizes. Equally, the association of forts with auxiliary units is not always clear cut. The late Roman writer Vegetius, perhaps drawing upon an earlier work by the Roman general Sextus Julius Frontinus (*c.* AD 40–103), explained the basic strategy behind the use of forts:

> Amongst the main duties of the commander, whether in camp or quartered in a town, is that he should ensure that pasturage for the animals, the supply of grain and other provisions, and access to water, firewood and fodder are all kept safe from attack by the enemy. This cannot otherwise be achieved unless *praesidia*, be they towns or walled *castella*, are situated in suitable places through which our supply line passes. If no existing fortification is available, *castella* surrounded by broad ditches are quickly constructed in suitable places. *Castella* are named from the diminutive word for camps. A number of infantry and cavalry stationed in them across the countryside maintain a safe route for the convoys. For it is only with difficulty that an enemy dares to approach those places in which he knows his adversaries are based, both ahead and behind.
>
> Vegetius, *Epitoma rei militaris* 3.8

CHRONOLOGY

27 BC–AD 14	**Reign of Augustus**
12–5 BC, AD 4–5	Roman armies campaign beyond the Rhine
AD 9	Varian disaster in Germany; occupation of Germany halted at left bank of the Rhine
AD 14–37	**Reign of Tiberius**
AD 15–16	Campaigns beyond the Rhine briefly resumed (Germanicus)
AD 37–41	**Reign of Gaius (Caligula)**
AD 41–54	**Reign of Claudius**
	Forts established on the German frontier along the Rhine (e.g. Valkenburg), and on the frontier of Raetia along the upper Danube (e.g. Oberstimm)
AD 43	Invasion of Britain; fort building in southern Britain to accommodate provincial garrison (e.g. Hod Hill)
AD 54–68	**Reign of Nero**
	Advance in Britain accompanied by new fort building (e.g. The Lunt, Nanstallon)
AD 69–79	**Reign of Vespasian**
	Advance in Britain and on Upper Rhine and Upper Danube accompanied by new fort building (e.g. Hofheim, Rottweil)
AD 79–81	**Reign of Titus**
	New forts built along Raetian frontier (e.g. Eining). In Britain, forts established in Wales (e.g. Pen Llystyn), northern England (e.g. Carlisle), southern Scotland (e.g. Newstead)
AD 81–96	**Reign of Domitian**
	Advance in Scotland accompanied by new fort building (e.g. Fendoch, Strageath). Establishment of Germania Inferior and Germania Superior as provinces. Minor adjustments on Upper Rhine and Upper Danube accompanied by new forts

	(e.g. Wiesbaden, Heidenheim). Separation of Moesia into M. Inferior and M. Superior; advance on Upper Danube accompanied by new forts (e.g. Künzing)
AD 98–117	**Reign of Trajan** Evacuation of Scotland accompanied by fort refurbishment in northern England (e.g. Vindolanda) and Wales (e.g. Gelligaer). Advance to Wetterau region in Germania Superior; small forts established along the Odenwald frontier (e.g. Hesselbach). Division of Pannonia into P. Inferior and P. Superior.
AD 101–03, 105–06	Dacian Wars. Forts established across the Danube in Dacia (e.g. Bumbeşti, Slăveni) and on the lower Danube (e.g. Ruse, Capidava).
AD 106	Annexation of Arabia. Presumed fort building (e.g. El-Humayma).
AD 117–38	**Reign of Hadrian** Establishment of continuous frontier works in Britain (Hadrian's Wall), Germania Superior and Raetia (timber palisade), accompanied by extensive fort building (e.g. Housesteads, Saalburg). Modification of Dacian frontier.
AD 138–61	**Reign of Antoninus Pius** Advance of frontiers in Britain (Antonine Wall), and in Upper Germany and Raetia, accompanied by extensive fort building (e.g. Balmuildy, Osterburken, Aalen).
AD 161–80	**Reign of Marcus Aurelius** Evacuation of Antonine Wall accompanied by fort refurbishment in southern Scotland and along Hadrian's Wall.
AD 167–75, 177–80	Marcomannic Wars.
AD 180–92	**Reign of Commodus** Damaged forts along Raetian and Pannonian frontier repaired (e.g. Böhming, Ellingen, Gerulata); new forts established on Rhine frontier (e.g. Niederbieber).
AD 193–211	**Reign of Septimius Severus** Continued care and maintenance of existing forts. Establishment of new forts on eastern (e.g. Qasr El-Hallabat) and African frontiers (e.g. Bu Njem). Trend towards heavier defences.
AD 211–17	**Reign of Caracalla**
AD 213	Campaign against the Alamanni
AD 222–35	**Reign of Severus Alexander** Forts in Upper Germany and Raetia repaired after incursions of the Alamanni (e.g. Zugmantel, Saalburg).
AD 253–68	**Reign of Gallienus**
AD 260	Abandonment of all forts east of the Rhine and north of the Danube (Agri Decumates).
AD 270–75	**Reign of Aurelian**
AD 271	Abandonment of all forts in Dacia.
AD 284–305	**Reign of Diocletian** Establishment of the Tetrarchy ('rule by four men'). Trend towards smaller, more heavily defended forts (e.g. Qasr Bshir)
AD 364–75	**Reign of Valentinian I** Hailed as the last great builder of fortifications.

CHRONOLOGY OF ROMAN AUXILIARY FORTS

The great battles of Republican Rome were fought by the legions, supported in many cases by allied troops providing the cavalry, archers and slingers that the legions lacked. For example, at Pharsalus in 48 BC, Pompey supplemented his legions with 1,200 slingers, 3,000 Cretan and Syrian archers, and 7,000 horsemen drawn from Thrace, Cappadocia, Macedonia and Syria. In the same engagement, Caesar's cavalry came mostly from Gaul. Over the next 20 years, Roman generals made increasing use of foreign troops to supply those arms in which the legions were deficient. Such troops gradually came to be known as the *auxilia*, or 'auxiliaries'.

When the emperor Augustus (27 BC–AD 14) set about rationalizing the army that would defend and extend the dominions of Rome, he settled upon a core of 28 legions assisted by a number of auxiliary units. Raised amongst the non-citizen *peregrini* of various warlike nations, there were units of Gauls, Spaniards and Syrians, and later Dacians and Britons, but Roman officers commanded all of them. The total numerical strength of these auxiliaries can only be estimated; even well-informed contemporaries had only a vague notion, and the tally will have fluctuated from generation to generation, in any case. The historian Tacitus, after recounting the whereabouts of the legions at the time of the emperor Tiberius (AD 14–37), wrote that the *auxilia* were 'not much inferior in strength, but it would be misleading to list them, as they moved here and there according to the needs of the moment, and increased or diminished in number' (Tac., *Ann.* 4.5).

Auxiliary forts under the Julio-Claudian emperors (27 BC–AD 68)

In his summary of Livy's *History*, the Hadrianic writer Florus records that more than 50 *castella* were established by Drusus, brother of the future emperor Tiberius, during campaigns against the German tribes in 11–9 BC (Florus 2.30). It was no doubt one of these forts that Tacitus meant when he wrote that the imperial prince Germanicus (Drusus's son), venturing across the Rhine again in AD 15, established a *castellum* on the site of his father's *praesidium* on Mons Taunus (Tac., *Ann.* 1.56).

Unfortunately, German archaeologists have so far identified only a handful of military sites dating from this time, and most have the character of large campaign bases that must have accommodated a composite force of legionaries and auxiliaries. For example, the early military base at Augsburg on the river Lech, in the province of Raetia (Switzerland), covers eight hectares or more, and indicates that a sizeable task force was stationed here. Similarly, the enormous 56ha fortress at Oberaden on the river Lippe, 70km east of the Rhine, surely held not only several legions, but a mix of auxiliaries as well; the excavator has suggested that these included troops from the Balkans and Asia, on the basis of finds such as the distinctively decorated *phalerae* (ornamental discs) and a wooden curved sword resembling the Thracian *sica*.

At this early stage in the development of the Roman Empire, troops were concentrated in army groups, poised to conquer new territories. For example, in AD 6, when Tiberius was massing an army for Augustus' planned invasion of the kingdom of the Marcomanni (modern Czech Republic), he assembled an enormous host, allegedly comprising ten legions, 14 allied cavalry units and 70 units of auxiliary infantry (Velleius 2.113.1). Later, in AD 9, the army of Augustus' ill-fated general Publius Quinctilius Varus, destroyed in the Teutoburg forest disaster, consisted of three legions, three cavalry units and six infantry units (Velleius 2.117.1). They would surely have characterized

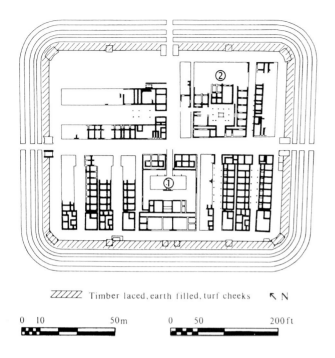

ZZZZZ Timber laced, earth filled, turf cheeks ↖ N

0 10   50m   0   50   200ft

Plan of the Phase II/III
(Claudian) fort at Valkenburg
(Netherlands). The *principia* (1)
is flanked by eight barracks,
while the *praetorium* (2)
is flanked by buildings
of uncertain use.
(© Author, after Hassall)

their base camp as a *castra*, rather than a *castellum* or even a *praesidium*.

However, smaller bases were established here and there, probably to fulfil specialized functions. In North Africa, during the reign of Tiberius, Roman troops were dispersed in forts to combat the Numidian threat posed by Tacfarinas, a time-served auxiliary turned brigand. On one occasion in AD 20, a Roman cohort, under attack in their *castellum*, abandoned their beleaguered commander and fled; as punishment, every tenth man was flogged to death, a precedent which encouraged other garrisons to stand firm (Tac., *Ann.* 3.20–21). Some years later, the general Publius Cornelius Dolabella surprised a Numidian war band 'at the partly ruined *castellum* named Auzea, which they themselves had earlier burnt' (Tac., *Ann.* 4.25). It is interesting to note that, even at this early stage of development, when affairs were still fairly fluid, the Romans named their forts for ease of identification.

Of course, the passage of Vegetius quoted above (p. 5) shows that troops could be quartered in towns. This seems to have been common in the urbanized provinces of the eastern Mediterranean, and explains Tacitus' comment that, on the arrival of Gnaeus Domitius Corbulo in Syria in AD 58, he found troops who 'stared at a rampart and ditch as if they were novel and astonishing' (Tac., *Ann.* 13.35). The same situation will have obtained in North Africa; the town of Thala in Numidia, for example, appears to have been garrisoned by auxiliary troops in AD 20 (Tac., *Ann.* 3.21). And a cohort was traditionally based in the Romanized south of Gaul as early as AD 21, not in a *castellum* but in the town of Lugdunum (Lyon, France) (Tac., *Ann.* 3.41). It is unclear whether the soldiers were simply billeted around the town, or whether they had their own military compound, like the one later found at Corbridge (England) or, later still, at Dura Europus (Syria). Similarly, garrisons could be planted in existing strongholds to watch the indigenous population. In 25 BC, when Augustus' general Gaius Petronius penetrated Nubia, 1,100km down the Nile, he planted a garrison of 400 men in the rocky cliff-top fortress of Premnis (Qasr Ibrim, Egypt). Similarly, a large three-hectare Roman fort was laid out in the corner of Hod Hill (England), a native hill fort captured during Claudius' invasion of Britain in AD 43. A few years later, perhaps under similar circumstances, the Romans installed a *praesidium* in the hill fort of Soza in the Crimean Bosphorus (Ukraine), 'because the temperament of the people was uncertain' (Tac., *Ann.* 12.16).

Where existing infrastructure was lacking, the Roman Army was obliged to build its own accommodation. In western Europe, archaeology has revealed early forts on the Lower Rhine at Vechten and Velsen (Netherlands), which probably held composite garrisons intended to support the Augustan–Tiberian campaigning in Germany. Velsen in particular has been identified with the '*castellum* named Flevum' (Tac., *Ann.* 4.72) which was attacked in AD 28 by the Frisians, over whose lands it maintained watch. The Roman garrison had been placed there, years earlier, to collect taxes; it is interesting that Tacitus characterizes the garrison as 'a band of citizens and allies' (*manus civium sociorumque*), which seems to indicate citizen legionaries as well as peregrine auxiliaries. This was perhaps the *praesidium* that Corbulo refortified in AD 47 (Tac., *Ann.* 11.19), when he was commander on the Rhine.

The 1.4ha fort at Valkenburg (Katwijk, Netherlands) is known to date from AD 39/40, when the emperor Gaius (Caligula, AD 37–41) visited the lower Rhine; an inscribed wooden tablet records the presence of a cohort of Gauls here (AE 1975, 633). The fort's Roman name, Praetorium Agrippinae, refers to the emperor's mother, the wife of Germanicus. The nearby fort at Roomburg (Netherlands) was probably built at the same time. On the Upper Rhine, Wiesbaden (Germany), opposite the legionary fortress at Mainz, was perhaps established in connection with the same emperor's planned invasion into the territory of the Chatti, and the first occupation at Hofheim, almost 20km farther east, dates from the reign of the emperor Claudius (AD 41–54).

So there was an early history of planting small garrisons in potentially hostile territory. The provision of stout defences and the securing of supply lines mitigated much of the risk. For example, the Augustan writer Strabo records how 'Petronius fortified Premnis better, threw in a garrison of 400 men and food for two years, and returned to Alexandria' (Strabo, *Geography* 17.1.54). But there was no sense in exposing a garrison to unnecessary danger. In AD 47, Claudius famously ordered Corbulo to withdraw his garrisons (*praesidia*) to the near side of the Rhine (Tac., *Ann.* 11.19), perhaps less out of jealousy (Cassius Dio 61.30.4–5) than the legitimate fear that he was stirring up trouble amongst the Germanic tribes. After all, Claudius' focus during these years was the conquest of southern Britain.

Other *praesidia* surely existed on the Upper Rhine at this time, if for no other reason than to offset the withdrawal of *legio II Augusta* from Strasbourg for the invasion of Britain. An early fort is known, for example, at Rheingönheim near Ludwigshafen, where the garrison could maintain a watch on the confluence of the rivers Rhine and Neckar. The famous encyclopaedist Pliny the Elder had served in the area as *praefectus alae* ('commander of a cavalry unit') under Claudius or Nero. As his nephew, Pliny the Younger, explained in a letter to his friend Baebius Macer (*Epist.* 3.5), his uncle had been inspired by the ghost of Drusus to write a 20-volume history of the German Wars (*Bella Germaniae*), during his stint in Germany. But it is his only surviving work, the *Naturalis Historia* (*Natural History*, dedicated to the emperor Titus), which contains clues suggesting that it was during Corbulo's governorship that Pliny's cavalry unit was stationed there. He also claimed that he had seen entire regiments sent out to capture wild geese (*Nat. Hist.* 10.27 & 54), which paints an interesting picture of army life there.

The reign of Claudius saw the establishment of Raetia (Switzerland) as a province. A few forts were constructed on the upper reaches of the Danube, from the headwaters at Hüfingen, 250km eastwards to Oberstimm. And, at least by the reign of Nero (AD 54–68), it seems that auxiliary garrisons were established at major crossings of the Danube in Noricum (Austria) and Pannonia (mostly Hungary), but archaeology has revealed only sketchy details. A legion,

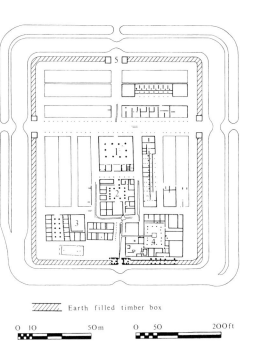

Earth filled timber box

0   10   50 m   0   50   200 ft

Plan of the Claudian fort at Oberstimm. In the central range, the *principia* (1) and *praetorium* (2) are flanked by barracks. A possible *valetudinarium* (3) lies in the *retentura*. The function of building (4) remains unknown. (© Author, after Hassall)

the *XV Apollinaris*, lay at Carnuntum (Deutsch Altenburg, Austria), facing the lands of the Suebic Germans. To the west, early forts were perhaps established in present-day Austria at Lentia (Linz), Lauriacum (Lorch), and Favianis (Mautern). To the east, an *ala Pannoniorum* lay about 65km downstream in the fort of Arrabona (Györ, Hungary), where it was soon replaced by the specialist horse-archers of *ala I Augusta Ituraeorum*. The deployment of cavalry in support of a legion is a recurring theme. Nero's Praetorian Prefect Nymphidius Sabinus had, earlier in his career, served as *praefectus alae* ('commander of a cavalry unit') at Szöny (Hungary), in the vicinity of the later legionary fortress of Brigetio, where he dedicated an altar (CIL 3, 4269).

Below the Danube bend, where the Roman Empire's neighbours were Sarmatian tribes, an early fort has been identified at Viziváros near Budapest (Hungary), predating the legionary fortress of Aquincum; it was garrisoned by an *ala I Hispanorum*. Other early forts lay at Lussonium (Dunakömlőd, Hungary) and Lugio (Dunaszekcső, Hungary), respectively 80km and 140km downstream. Their positions seem a little exposed, with the nearest legion, *XIII Gemina*, well to the rear at Poetovio (Ptuj, Slovenia). But their primary purpose was simply to watch the river crossings, and their garrisons probably had a sizeable cavalry element to assist in patrolling.

On the lower Danube, a legion, *V Macedonica*, had been based at Oescus (Gigen, Bulgaria) under Augustus, perhaps brigaded with *ala Pansiana* to facilitate long-range patrolling (though some have doubted the existence of this unit, mentioned only on the fragmentary AE 1960, 12). A second legion, *IV Scythica*, lay in the Moesian hinterland, perhaps at Naissus (Niš, Serbia), supported by auxiliaries at Timacum Minus (Ravna, Croatia), on the road up to the later fortress at Ratiaria (Archar, Bulgaria). But Claudius' annexation of Thrace in AD 45 and the mass movement, around the same time, of trans-Danubian tribes initiated a series of transfers. A third legion, *VIII Augusta*, arrived on the river at Novae (Steklen, Bulgaria), and with the departure of *IV Scythica* early in Nero's reign a new fortress was built for *VII Claudia* at Viminacium (Kostolac, Serbia). (For the movements of the legions, see Fortress 43: *Roman Legionary Fortresses 27 BC–AD 378* (Osprey

Reconstructed gateway at The Lunt Roman fort, Baginton (England). (© The Lunt Roman Fort / Coventry Heritage and Arts Trust Ltd)

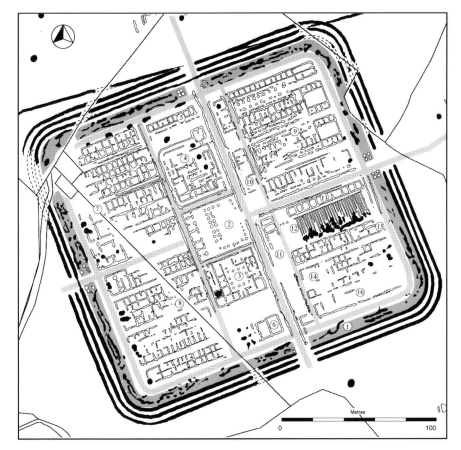

Plot of a gradiometer survey of the 3.8ha fort site at Llanfor (Wales). Nothing can be seen above ground, but the survey shows the single-period (probably Flavian) fort in astonishing detail. The standard buildings are easily picked out; e.g., the granary (12) with its parallel floor supports. (Survey by David Hopewell (Gwynedd Archaeological Trust) and John Burman (Meirioneth Geophysical Survey Team). © Dave Hopewell)

Publishing Ltd: Oxford, 2006) by the same author.) Cavalry support cannot be proved, but auxiliary *alae* have been suggested at Augustae (Harlets) and Utum (Milkovica) in present-day Bulgaria. Structural evidence for these is lacking, but early forts are known in present-day Serbia at Novae (Brnjica-Gradac), Taliata (Donji Milanovac), and Diana (Davidovac-Karataš). All of these would have been well placed to control river crossings.

Auxiliary units were also stationed in northern Spain at this time. An inscription from Soto la Vega, for example, records the 'boundary of the lands of the Fourth Cohort of Gauls, between the Fourth Cohort of Gauls and the town of Bedunia' (*terminus pratorum cohortis IIII Gallorum inter cohors IIII Gallorum et civitatem Beduniensium*: AE 1961, 345) under the Julio-Claudian emperors. Four different regiments are known to have borne this name, but it is likely to have been the *cohors IIII Gallorum equitata* that later appears in Britain from the time of Hadrian onwards; such long-range transfers were not uncommon.

Garrisons were being planted in the east, too. Tacitus records that, in AD 51, the *castellum* of Gorneae in Armenia was under the command of the *praefectus* Caelius Pollio and a centurion named Casperius (Tac., *Ann.* 12.45-46). The dual command may be a hint of a composite garrison. Certainly, when Corbulo arrived in AD 58, he is said to have punished two *alae* and three cohorts by denying them the sanctuary of their fort, which was named Initia. Instead, he forced them to encamp *extra vallum* ('outside the rampart') until they had rehabilitated themselves *prosperis excursionibus* ('through successful raiding') (Frontin., *Strat.* 4.1.21; cf. Tac., *Ann.* 13.36, for cavalry *castella*). The fort was

The left *praetentura* of the fort at Valkenburg (Netherlands) during excavation in 1941. The foundations of barrack blocks can be seen, incorporating timber sleeper beams. The uprights were broken off during the Roman dismantling of the fort in preparation for refurbishment. (© Provinzie Zuid Holland)

clearly a large one to accommodate this mixed garrison. The writer Josephus uses the word *stratopedon* ('camp') to describe the forts established at Jericho and Adida by Vespasian, on his way to besiege Jerusalem in AD 68. These, too, must have been large, as 'he placed in each one a garrison made up of Romans and allies' (Joseph., *BJ* 4.486), which recalls the mixed garrison of Flevum. But on the other hand, 'the *castellum* named Arsamosata' in Armenia was garrisoned by a single cohort (Tac., *Ann.* 15.10). Several regiments have left epigraphic traces from this time, but we have no structural evidence of their bases.

In Britain, a sizeable auxiliary garrison required winter accommodation when they were not actively campaigning. By AD 60, legionary fortresses had been established for *II Augusta* at Isca (Exeter, England), *IX Hispana* at Lindum (Lincoln, England), and *XIV Gemina* and *XX Valeria Victrix* probably in the Gloucester area, where large bases are known at Usk and Kingsholm. Many forts date from this period, but few are known in detail. Two exceptions are The Lunt (Baginton, England), where an early 1.5ha turf-and-timber fort had many of its internal buildings refurbished in stone, and Nanstallon (Devon, England), where the tiny 0.9ha fort perhaps held only part of a unit.

Auxiliary forts under Vespasian and Titus (AD 69–81)

Our earliest archaeological evidence for the systematic placing of auxiliary units in their own permanent forts dates from the Flavian period. It is only from that time that we find evidence of individual units garrisoning permanent stations at strategic points, mostly around the periphery of the empire, and these gradually formed the garrisons of the imperial frontiers.

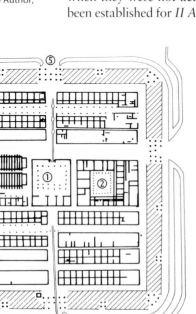

Plan of the fort at Pen Llystyn. The central range is occupied by (1) the *principia*, (2) the *praetorium*, (3) a pair of granaries and (4) a store building. The *porta praetoria* (5) faces south-west. (© Author, after Hassall)

The forts of the western provinces in particular were largely constructed using earth, turf and timber. These were not considered to be temporary building materials. In fact, a length of rampart with timber gateway erected as an archaeological experiment in 1970 at the fort of The Lunt was still standing in the 1990s, and only required major refurbishment in 2004. Thus, by the reign of Vespasian (AD 69–79), the earth-and-timber forts erected in the AD 40s and 50s would have been ready for a thoroughgoing programme of repairs. Others damaged or destroyed in the fighting that followed Nero's death required a total rebuild. The fort at Valkenburg on the lower Rhine, for example, was rebuilt at this time, again using turf and timber materials, but the builders took the opportunity to rearrange the internal buildings. Often, it seems that a change of garrison could precipitate a complete remodelling of the facilities, creating a layer of destruction deposits that are superficially similar to the effects of enemy action. Archaeology has also revealed a growing tendency towards greater uniformity in fort layout, although no two forts from any period of Roman history are ever exactly alike.

New forts were built on the Upper Rhine under Vespasian. In the Wetterau region, a small fort named Castellum Mattiacorum (Mainz-Kastell) was erected opposite the Mainz legionary fortress. From there, Roman control extended north-east along the river Nidda, with garrisons at Hofheim, Heddernheim (Frankfurt), Okarben and Friedberg. At the same time, further south, isolated garrisons were planted across the Rhine at Groß-Gerau and along the lower Neckar at Ladenburg (Roman Lopodunum) and Heidelberg. Further south again, a road struck east from Strasbourg, through the Schwarzwald and along the upper reaches of the Neckar, before heading east towards the Danube. A milestone found at Offenburg (CIL 13, 9082) dates the work to AD 74. The lands of the upper Neckar, which Tacitus calls the Agri Decumates (Tac., *Germ.* 29), were secured by new forts at Sultz, Waldmössingen and Rottweil, far in advance of the legionary fortress of Vindonissa (Windisch). Simultaneously, new forts were established on the upper Danube in Raetia. For example, at Günzburg, a dedication set up by a *praefectus equitum* ('commander of cavalry') may be evidence of construction in stone during the years AD 77–78 (AE 1911, 228), while under Titus, a turf-and-timber fort was erected at Abusina (Eining, Germany).

Along the Danube proper, the Julio-Claudian foundations continued in occupation, while others were steadily added. In Noricum (Austria), the new earth-and-timber forts of Augustiana (Traismauer) and Comagena (Tulln) accommodated more cavalry in the form of *ala I Augusta Thracum* and *ala I Commagenorum*. Forts were probably also established now at Zwentendorf, Wallsee and Zeiselmauer, but their garrisons are unknown. In Pannonia, the legionary garrison at Carnuntum was bolstered now (if not earlier) by the building of a fort at nearby Petronell for *ala I Hispanorum Aravacorum*, and another at Klosterneuburg, 50km upstream, for *cohors*

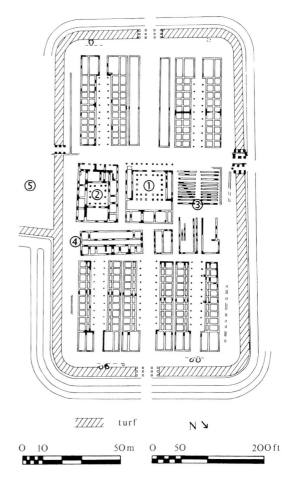

Plan of the fort at Fendoch. The central range contains (1) the *principia*, (2) the *praetorium* and (3) a pair of granaries. Building (4) is thought to be a *valetudinarium*. The fort has an annexe (5) on the south-east side. (© Author, after Hassall)

turf   N ↘

0 10   50m   0   50   200 ft

Tacitus records how, in Autumn AD 69, Julius Civilis, a renegade auxiliary officer and chieftain of the Batavians, began to foment rebellion on the Lower Rhine. The tribe of the Canninefates, who lived along the North Sea coast, made common cause with their Batavian neighbours, and fell upon a Roman fort near the shore. The attack was sudden and unexpected, and the fort was destroyed and looted. Several Roman forts have produced evidence of destruction at this time, most famously Valkenburg, where excavations from 1941 until 1967 revealed six chronological phases spanning almost 300 years.

I Montanorum. Further downstream, at the Danube bend, a large dedication slab from the early fort at Obuda (Budapest) shows that *ala I Tungrorum Frontoniana* was already present in AD 73 (AE 1993, 1307). On the long southern stretch of the Danube through present-day Hungary, the two existing forts of Lussonium and Lugio were joined by a third, named Intercisa, 40km north at Dunaújváros (Hungary) for *ala II Asturum*, and a fourth, Teutoburgium, 80km south at Dalj (Croatia) for *ala II Hispanorum Aravacorum*. The next Flavian fort lies about 120km farther on, at Acumincum (Stari Slankamen, Serbia), where *cohors I Britannica equitata* was based. Clearly, with such wide spacing, there was no question of a closed frontier; rather, Acumincum was strategically sited at the precise spot where the major river Tisza flows south into the Danube. These forts were designed to maintain a watch on the lands beyond the river.

In neighbouring Moesia, it is likely that, alongside the legionary fortress at Viminacium and the early forts at Novae, Taliata and Diana, others were founded at Tekija, Kostol (where tile-stamps of *cohors III Brittonum* are known) and Brza Palanka. One of these perhaps housed the specialist archers of *cohors I Cretum*. Early Flavian occupation has also been suggested at Pojejena (Romania) on the left bank, perhaps by *cohors V Gallorum*.

The focus in these years lay in Britain, where successive governors pushed north, consolidating as they went. A pattern of forts spread across Wales and northern England to accommodate the province's large auxiliary garrison; Pen Llystyn (Wales), now sadly destroyed by quarrying, provides a good example of a complete fort plan from these years. The beginnings of a road network provided communications with new legionary fortresses in the rear at Isca (Caerleon, Wales), Deva (Chester, England) and Eburacum (York, England), as well as forward bases at Carlisle, Corbridge and Newstead.

Auxiliary forts under Domitian (AD 81–96)

In Britain under Domitian, the armies pressed on into Scotland, creating a web of garrisons right up to the Forth–Clyde isthmus, and a line of forts running broadly north-east from Camelon, via Ardoch, Strageath and Bertha, to a new legionary fortress at Inchtuthil, and on to Cardean and Stracathro. A second line, offset to the north, ran from Drumquassle, via Bochastle and Dalginross, to Fendoch, each sited at the mouth of a Highland glen. The garrisons of all but one remain unknown, but Ardoch, at 3.5ha, was more than large enough for the *cohors I Hispanorum*

Plan of the fort at Drobeta (Romania). The central *principia* (1) is flanked by two granaries (3) and two courtyard buildings (2) of uncertain use. If the fort held two units, these may be the *praetoria* of the two commanders. (© Author, after Hassall)

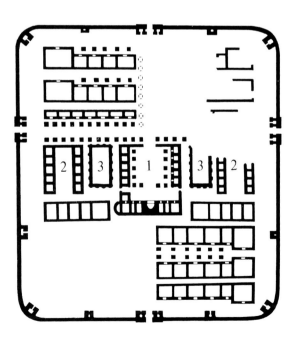

Stone wall with earth bank?

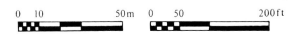

attested there (RIB 2213), prompting the suggestion that there may have been legionaries billeted here as well.

In AD 83–85, Domitian was personally based at Mainz to supervise the war against the Chatti, which had probably been engineered to boost the new emperor's military prestige. The 2.2ha fort at Wiesbaden was now rebuilt in stone by *cohors II Raetorum* (CIL 13, 7583–84), before their move to Butzbach around AD 90. Their replacements, *cohors III Dalmatarum* (ILS 2561), were busy during the Trajanic consolidation of the Main Valley; tiles produced in their tile-works are found at Oberscheidenthal, Groß-Krotzenburg and Rückingen, as well as at Wiesbaden. Tile-stamps attest the presence of the formidable *cohors I Flavia Damascenorum milliaria equitata sagittariorum*, a 1,000-strong part-mounted archer unit, at the four-hectare fort of Friedberg. Further north, other forts were established on the left bank of the Rhine. At Heddesdorf, a 2.8ha stone fort was probably built around this time for *cohors II Hispanorum equitata*, moving up from Rottweil, and at Niederberg, opposite the confluence of Mosel and Rhine, a fort of similar size was built for *cohors VII Raetorum equitata*. Across the border in Lower Germany, a new fort was planted for *ala Noricorum* at Dormagen, where the excavation of the barracks brought to light the horses' urine pits. There is an interesting story that, when Domitian constructed forts in the territory of the Cubii in AD 83, he recompensed the natives for any crops which they had lost to his fort builders (Frontin., *Strat.* 2.11.7).

But the focus quickly shifted to the Danube. As the Pannonian frontier came under increasing stress, *ala I Flavia Britannica*, one of the first milliary cavalry units to be created, was established at Vienna as a precursor to the later legionary fortress of Vindobona. *Ala I Cannanefatium* was stationed at Gerulata (Rusovec, Slovakia), 70km downstream, where it was to remain well into the next century, and the fort of Solva was established at Esztergom (Hungary). All three faced into the territory of the Suebic Germans.

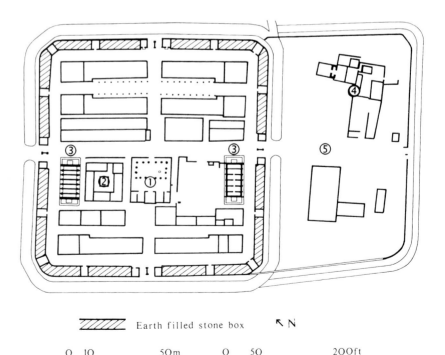

Plan of Gelligaer II (Wales). Barracks and store buildings fill the *praetentura* and *retentura*, while the central range has the standard *principia* (1), *praetorium* (2) and granaries (3). The bathhouse (4) is situated in the fort annexe (5). (© Author, after Hassall)

Earth filled stone box   N

0   10   50m   0   50   200ft

On the outbreak of war with the Dacians in AD 86, Moesia was divided into two provinces. In a move that foreshadowed the similar treatment of the Rhine command, Domitian created a province of Upper Moesia, with a new fortress at Singidunum (Belgrade, Serbia) joining the existing fortress at Viminacium; and a province of Lower Moesia, with fortresses at Novae and Oescus. The reason was perhaps in order to bring the talents of two experienced consular governors to a sector normally governed by one. There were massive troop movements, which entailed (or were caused by) the evacuation of Scotland and the abandonment of the Inchtuthil fortress. New forts were established in Lower Moesia at Silistra (Bulgaria), the site of the later fortress of Durostorum, and in Upper Moesia, including one just across the Danube at Drobeta (Turnu Severin, Romania), which became the bridgehead for Trajan's invasion of Dacia.

In Raetia, around AD 90, no doubt in connection with further action against the Suebi, the 5.2ha fort of Heidenheim was built in stone for *ala II Flavia milliaria*, moving up beyond the Danube from Günzburg and doubling in size at the same time.

Stone wall with earth bank ↖ N

0 10 50m 0 50 200 ft

Plan of the fort at Chesters (England). The numbered features are: (1) the *principia*, (2) the *praetorium*, (3) a pair of granaries and (4) the *porta praetoria*. (© Author, after Hassall)

Auxiliary forts under Trajan (AD 98–117)

Trajan is famous above all for his annexation of Dacia (Transylvania in modern Romania), following his Dacian Wars (AD 101–02 and 105–06), but there were developments on other frontiers as well. In Britain, the garrisons had gradually fallen back, first to the area around Newstead, and finally, by the early years of the 2nd century AD, to the Tyne–Solway isthmus and the forts along the line of the Stanegate road. Fort building continued elsewhere, for example at Gelligaer (RIB 397), where a new stone-built fort was erected on a different site from its vacated Flavian predecessor, indicating a change of garrison.

Trajan's new province of Dacia entailed widespread construction, as a network of forts was established, linking back to the Danube at Viminacium (*legio VII Claudia*'s fortress) in Moesia Superior, and at Novae (*legio I Italica*'s fortress) and Durostorum (*legio XI Claudia*'s new fortress) in Moesia Inferior. In addition, on the main road north from Drobeta, *cohors IV Cypria* was stationed at Bumbeşti, halfway to the *XIII Gemina*'s new fortress at Apulum (Alba Julia). To the west, a route crossed the Banat from Viminacium via forts at Arcidava (Varadia) and Tibiscum (Jupa). To the east, a route ran north from Novae, following the River Olt, with garrisons at Slăveni and Buridava

B   ZUGMANTEL FORT AND EXTERNAL SETTLEMENT (*VICUS*), c. AD 200

Where forts were occupied for a lengthy period, a civil settlement (or *vicus*) often grew up outside the ramparts. The annexes found outside many forts may be the precursor to such settlements. The fort at Zugmantel lies on the Taunus Ridge on the Upper German frontier. It was originally established as a timber construction around AD 90 and was refurbished during the reign of Hadrian; the stone fort only dates from the mid-2nd century AD, with a final

remodelling in AD 223 creating the 2.1ha fort that was home to *cohors I Treverorum equitata*. It was finally given up, along with the other forts on the Taunus, in AD 260. The main part of the *vicus* extended from the fort's *porta praetoria* south-east along the road to the garrison bathhouse. The site is known from extensive excavations, which ran from 1894 into the 20th century. It is heavily forested and nothing is now visible.

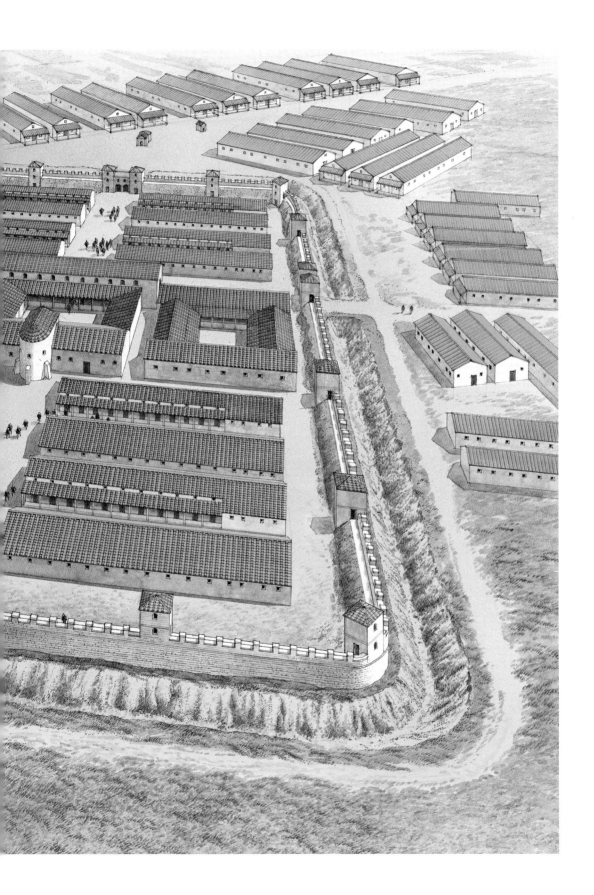

(Stolniceni). And still further east, another route went north from Durostorum via Drajna de Sus and Breţcu. Finally, an arc of forts was established in the north of Dacia, with garrisons at Resculum (Bologa), Buciumi, Largiana (Romanaşi), Porolissum (Moigrad), Samum (Caşei), Ilişua and elsewhere.

The focus on Dacia probably drew attention to the situation on the lower Danube, which remained completely ungarrisoned. Having established *legio XI Claudia* at Durostorum (Silistra, Bulgaria), Trajan ordered the riverside forts of Sexaginta Prisca (Ruse, Bulgaria) and Appiaria (Rjahovo, Bulgaria) to be constructed on the same sector. And, with the stationing of *legio V Macedonica* far down the river at Troesmis (Iglita, Romania), further forts were established at Capidava and Barboşi (Romania).

The late Roman historian Eutropius believed that Trajan had founded towns (*urbes*) across the Rhine in Germany (Eutrop. 8.2), but this is surely a mistaken reference to the establishment of forts on the line now familiar as the 'Obergermanische–Raetischer Limes' (or ORL). In the Wetterau region of Upper Germany, a chain of new forts was built, with garrisons at Butzbach, Echzell, Altenstadt, Marköbel, Rückingen and Groß-Krotzenburg. Further forts were built on the so-called Odenwald *limes*, running south to the upper Neckar, including the small forts at Eulbach, Würzberg, Hesselbach and Schlossau. This advance has been linked with the successful conquest of Dacia and the resultant need to redistribute the auxiliary troops that had been raised for the long wars there.

In AD 106 the Nabatean kingdom was absorbed into the Roman Empire as the province of Arabia. Unfortunately, in common with the rest of the eastern frontier, few fort sites can be identified. For example, *cohors I Thebaeorum* is known to have been involved in the annexation, but its subsequent whereabouts remain a mystery. A notable exception is provided by the site of El-Humayma (Jordan), known to the Romans as Hauara, where a perfectly rectangular three-hectare Trajanic fort has been investigated. The situation in North Africa is similarly vague, but building inscriptions from the 2.4ha fort of Ad Majores (Algeria) date from AD 105 (CIL 8, 2478–79).

Auxiliary forts under Hadrian (AD 117–38)
We reach a period of welcome stability under Hadrian, when the emphasis shifts from conquest to consolidation. Along with the increasing body of epigraphic (inscriptional) evidence, this gives us our best chance of assigning individual units to provincial armies, although we still lack the refinements that would allow the universal identification of particular fort garrisons. An important study by the epigrapher Paul Holder has assembled the evidence for the whereabouts of over 500 auxiliary units at this time, and it remains for future scholars to explore their assignment to known archaeological sites.

Important developments under Hadrian include the building of Hadrian's Wall (England) and its associated stone forts, with fine examples at Housesteads, Chesters and Wallsend. There were evidently further refinements along the Upper German and Raetian frontiers, and new forts continued to be built, for example, at Zugmantel and Saalburg. The boundary of Trajan's new province of Dacia was subtly altered as well, by drawing the eastern frontier within the Carpathians to create a more unified entity. At the same time, some of Trajan's forts were refurbished, for example, at Resculum, where the rebuilding was probably occasioned (as was often the case) by a change of garrison.

Of course, the perennial round of maintenance and refurbishment continued. The deployment of new units and the transfer of existing ones required fort

The 1.6ha fort at Welzheim-Ost lies on the outer *limes* of Upper Germany, and was built facing the large cavalry fort of Welzheim-West, 500m away. The garrison was a *numerus Brittonum*. (© Dietwulf Baatz)

construction. Rapidum and Praesidium Sufative (Algeria) were amongst several new forts constructed in Mauretania in the AD 120s (e.g. CIL 8, 20833; AE 1985, 984).

Auxiliary forts under the Antonines: Antoninus Pius (AD 138–61)

Whereas we have Tacitus for the Julio-Claudians and Josephus for the Flavians, the paucity of written sources for the Antonine emperors makes it more difficult to construct a continuous narrative of events. The reign of Antoninus Pius was generally hailed as a time of peace, although warfare in Britain culminated, around AD 140, in the building of the Antonine Wall (Scotland) and its associated turf-and-timber forts (e.g. Rough Castle and Bar Hill, and two stone-built examples at Balmuildy and Castlecary). The occupation of Lowland Scotland entailed much fort building, often on or near the site of Flavian works (e.g. the 1.1ha fort at Crawford, overlying a 0.8ha Flavian fort). Again, the kingpin of the fort network lay at Newstead, where a 5.9ha fort overlay its Flavian predecessor. In the later AD 150s, there was also a further advance of troops in Upper Germany and Raetia to the so-called 'outer *limes*', including forts at Osterburken, Welzheim and Aalen. The need for attention on this frontier was perhaps a contributory factor in the decision to abandon the Antonine Wall in around AD 160.

Auxiliary forts under the Antonines: Marcus Aurelius and Commodus (AD 161–92)

Warfare plagued the reign of Marcus Aurelius, the philosopher emperor. First, the Chatti caused trouble in the Wetterau, with possible destruction around Echzell. Then the long drawn-out Marcomannic Wars threatened Pannonia, drawing the emperor to Carnuntum to direct affairs in person. Although the reign of Commodus saw further warfare in Britain, the AD 180s were largely years of refurbishment; individual garrisons saw to their water supply, for example, as at Öhringen, or rebuilt their fort defences in stone, as at Ellingen. A rare example of a new fort established at this time is the 5.2ha fort of Niederbieber (Germany); the little 0.7ha fort at Böhming was perhaps a new foundation, too. Meanwhile, rebuilding at the likes of Gerulata can probably be put down to the destruction wrought by the Alamanni on the Pannonian frontier.

The Antonine frontiers

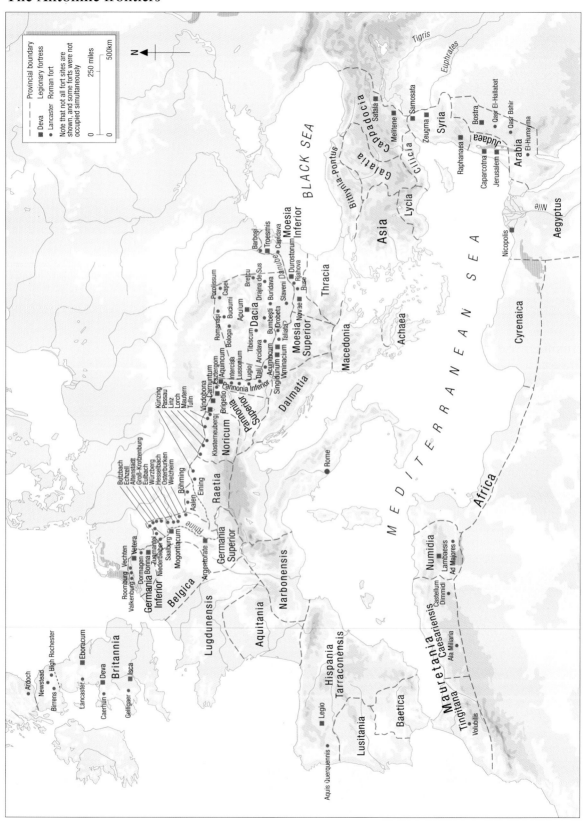

Provincial boundary
Legionary fortress
Deva Lancaster Roman fort

Note that not all fort sites are shown, and some forts were not occupied simultaneously

N

0   250 miles
0   500km

Tigris
Euphrates

Satala
Melitene Samosata
Cappadocia Zeugma Qasr El-Hallabat
Galatia Syria Bostra Qasr Bshir
Raphanaea Arabia
Asia Lycia Caparcotna El-Humayma
Cilicia Judaea
Jerusalem

Nile
Aegyptus

BLACK SEA

Bithynia-Pontus

Barbosi
Troesmis
Bretju Capidava Moesia
Pozojissum Drajna de Sus Slaveni Durostorum Inferior
Casei Buridava Rjahova
Romanasi Apulum Bumbesti Orobeta Buse Thracia
Bologa Tibiscum Taliata? Novae
Tibiscum Arcidava Moesia
Dacia Acumbucm Superior
Lugio Dalj Singidunum
Intercisa Lussonium Viminacium
Aquincum Dalmatia
Esztergom Aquincum
Carnuntum Pannonia Inferior
Vindobona Brigetio
Künzing Klosterneuburg
Passau Sabaria
Linz
Lorch Pannonia
Mautern Superior
Tulln Noricum

MEDITERRANEAN SEA

Macedonia Achaea

Cyrenaica

Butzbach
Echzell Raetia
Altenstadt
Groß-Krotzenburg
Eulbach Böhming
Würzberg Aalen
Hesselbach Eining
Osterburken
Welzheim

Rome

Roomburg Vechten
Valkenburg Dormagen Vetera
Zugmantel
Saalburg Bonna
Mogontiacum
Niederbieber
Germania
Inferior Argentorate Germania
Superior
Belgica Narbonensis
Rhine

Africa

Numidia
Lambaesis
Ad Majores
Castellum Dimmidi
Mauretania Caesariensis
Ala Miliaria

Ardoch
Newstead High Rochester
Birrens Eboracum
Lancaster Deva Britannia
Caerhun Isca
Gelligaer

Lugdunensis

Aquitania

Hispania
Tarraconensis

Baetica

Legio

Lusitania

Tingitana
Volubilis

Aquis Querquennis

22

Auxiliary forts under the Severans: Septimius Severus, Caracalla and Severus Alexander (AD 193–235)

After years of civil war and campaigning against Parthia, the reign of Septimius Severus saw further refurbishment of existing fortifications, as well as new foundations in Africa and the east. In Mauretania Caesariensis, the aptly named fort of Ala Milliaria (Benian, Algeria) probably dates from this time (AE 1902, 4), as does the irregularly shaped fort of Castellum Dimmidi (Messad, Algeria: AE 1948, 214). The so-called oasis forts in Tripolitania (Libya), at Gheria el-Garbia, Ghadames, and Bu Njem (CIL 8, 10992), are also Severan foundations.

Meanwhile, in the province of Arabia, a very small 0.25ha enclosure at Qasr El-Uweinid (Jordan) was apparently constructed as a 'new Severan fort' (*castellum novum Severianum*: AE 1978, 827) around AD 200. And in AD 213, at the even smaller 0.13ha blockhouse of Qasr El-Hallabat (Jordan), men from four different units 'built the new fort' (*castellum novum aedificaverunt milites cohortium VI Hispanorum I Thracum V Afrorum Severianae III Thracum*: Kennedy 2000, 93). It is interesting to note that the Romans appear to have classified these sites as *castella*; indeed, some have doubted that the inscriptions truly refer to these tiny fortifications, suggesting that they may have been salvaged from elsewhere for re-use by the Severan builders. In general, archaeologists classify such small fortifications as 'fortlets', but the defining characteristic is the absence of a headquarters building, which indicates that the site could not function independently.

On other frontiers, such a small fortification would have been called a *burgus*. For example, in around AD 215, the governor of Numidia 'ordered the *burgus* of the Antonine scouts to be built' (*burgum speculatorium Antoninianorum ... legatus ... fieri iussit*: ILS 2636), referring to the 0.16ha blockhouse at El Kantara (Tunisia). A century earlier, on the Odenwald *limes* of Upper Germany, the garrison of the Schneidershecke watchtower (Wp. 10/37) dedicated an altar to Jupiter 'because of the completion of the *burgus*'

Ruins of the *porta principalis sinistra* on the north-east side of the fort at Gheria el-Garbia (Libya) viewed from the fort interior. The window is on an upper level of the gate tower. (© Jona Lendering)

(*ob burgum explicitum*: ILS 2614). Confusingly, an inscription thought to have come not from a tower but from the 2.8ha Severan fort at Gheria el-Garbia, records that the commander of a legionary vexillation 'erected the *burgus* from the ground by means of the same vexillation' (*burgum a solo per eandem vexillationem instituit*: CIL 8, 3); despite the grand size of the inscription, it is more likely to have belonged to the nearby 0.1ha blockhouse at Gheria esh-Shergia.

Meanwhile, on the Upper German and Raetian frontier, a generation of Alamanni were cowed by Roman campaiging under Caracalla. Consequently, rebuilding at Zugmantel in AD 223 under Severus Alexander (CIL 13, 7612) was perhaps simply general maintenance. Most forts were maintained well into the mid-3rd century AD, when the abandonment of the Agri Decumates and the province of Dacia occasioned a withdrawal back to the line of the Flavian frontiers.

THE DESIGN AND DEVELOPMENT OF AUXILIARY FORTS

The strength and organization of auxiliary units

A combination of evidence shows that Roman auxiliary units were organized into three basic types: the infantry cohort (*cohors peditata*), the cavalry squadron (*ala*), and the equitate cohort (*cohors equitata*), which modern writers sometimes call 'part-mounted'. Each of these three types is found as a standard unit, nominally 500 strong (which the Romans called *quingenaria*), or as an enlarged unit, nominally 1,000 strong (*milliaria*). Of course, it is likely that, in common with army units in all periods of history, the actual strength varied with patterns of recruitment and wartime losses. But it seems that the terms 'quingenary' and 'milliary' were never intended literally, and could only ever have served as approximations.

When it comes to the detailed breakdown of auxiliary units, we rely upon an ancient tract known as the *Liber de munitionibus castrorum* (*Book about camp fortifications*), attributed to a writer called Hyginus. This work is something of an enigma, for it is well known that both the title and the author are later additions to an untitled, anonymous tract. But it is convenient to continue referring to it by the commonly accepted author and title. The army that it describes is also undated, but there is broad agreement that it must derive from the 2nd century AD. Within that period, the reigns of Trajan and Marcus Aurelius both have their supporters.

Hyginus' purpose was to calculate the space required in a temporary camp for each type of unit. He records that the *ala milliaria* ('milliary squadron') was subdivided into 24 *turmae* ('troops'), each officered by three men: a *decurio* ('decurion'), a *duplicarius* ('double-pay man'), and a *sesquiplicarius* ('pay-and-a-half man'). He further claims that there were 1,000 horses, one per trooper, with three for each decurion, and two for each of the other officers (*De mun. castr.* 16). However, subtracting these extra 96 officers' mounts (four per *turma*) leaves horses for 832 men, a number not easily divided into 24 *turmae*. Hyginus goes on to describe the *ala quingenaria* ('quingenary squadron') as having 16 *turmae* ('troops'); he omits the total number of horses, but confirms that there were 64 extra for the officers (again, four per *turma*).

We can turn to another, rather less enigmatic, source at this point. Hadrian's friend Arrian, who governed the frontier province of Cappadocia for several years, wrote a number of books on a military theme. One of these, entitled the *Tactica* (*Tactics*), contains the information that a quingenary *ala* numbered 512 troopers (Arrian, *Tact.* 18). This total has the virtue of being exactly divisible by 16, the expected number of *turmae* in the *ala*, and suggests that each *turma* consisted of 32 men; it may be significant that Vegetius' legionary cavalry was divided into troops of 32 (Veg., *Epit.* 2.14). Arrian's total of 512 men seems close enough to the notional 500 in order to merit the term *quingenaria*. But there are problems when his arithmetic is applied to the milliary *ala*, because 24 *turmae* of 32 men gives a total of 768, well below the notional 1,000. Nor does it square with Hyginus' figure of 832 horses. Until further evidence comes to light, we should perhaps envisage the milliary *ala* as roughly one-and-a-half times as big as the standard unit.

The infantry cohorts present a simpler proposition. The quingenary version was modelled on the legionary cohort, and consisted of six *centuriae* ('centuries'), each probably of 80 men giving a total of 480 effectives. The addition of two or three officers in each century brings the total to almost 500. The milliary cohort, on the other hand, consisted of ten *centuriae* (Hyg., *De mun. castr.* 28).

The third unit type, the equitate cohort, included a mounted contingent in addition to the standard infantry centuries. Modern writers have assumed that the basic infantry units (six *centuriae* in a quingenary unit, and ten *centuriae* in a milliary unit) were augmented by, respectively, four *turmae* and eight *turmae* of cavalry. But Hyginus records, rather precisely, that the milliary version contained 760 infantrymen (a figure which gives *centuriae* of 76 men, rather than the expected 80) and 240 cavalry troopers, which (distributed amongst eight *turmae*) gives a troop strength of 30 men (*De mun. castr.* 26). The quingenary version was half this size.

A fourth type of unit, simply called a *numerus* ('unit'), appears towards the end of the 1st century AD. Classified by their ethnic origin, these *numeri* appear to have been raised amongst peoples on the fringes of the empire, perhaps to exploit their exotic fighting skills. Their official titles often incorporate a geographical element, indicating their current or previous station, as for example *numerus Palmyrenorum Porolissensium sagittariorum* ('unit of Porolissensian archers from Palmyra': AE 1944, 56) based at Porolissum (Moigrad, Romania).

Small fort at Hesselbach, c. AD 100

The fort at Hesselbach lies in the Odenwald, where the Upper German frontier ran from the reign of Trajan until the advance to the 'outer *limes*' under Antoninus Pius. Excavations in 1964–66 recovered a complete ground plan, illustrating a full Roman fort in miniature. In particular, the presence of a *principia* (headquarters building) demonstrates that the fort was under an independent command, and the garrison was not simply outposted from elsewhere. Hesselbach is often called a '*numerus* fort', because in Upper Germany these small forts are associated with the army units known as *numeri*, although this association is not necessarily found in other provinces.

The size and internal structure of these units remain a mystery, but some were evidently large enough for dispersal across several locations. For example, in Upper Germany, *numerus Brittonum Triputiensium* appears to have been distributed amongst several small 0.6ha forts in the same sector of the Odenwald *limes*, including Eulbach (CIL 13, 6518) and Hesselbach (CIL 13, 6514); each fort was under the command of a legionary centurion, who was seconded for the purpose. On the other hand, *numerus exploratorum Germanicianorum Divitiensium* was perhaps concentrated at Niederbieber during the reign of Commodus (CIL 13, 7751), as it was commanded by a senior *praefectus* who would normally have commanded a milliary unit. Other *numeri* were evidently small enough to be brigaded alongside regular units, as in the case of *numerus exploratorum Bremeniensium*, who shared the fort at Bremenium (High Rochester, England) with *cohors I fida Vardullorum equitata* (RIB 1262).

These are the basic units of Roman troops that we find garrisoned in the forts of the empire. Archaeologists often assume that a single *centuria* and its officers, or two *turmae* and their officers, occupied a single barrack block, and furthermore that eight men invariably shared a room. This is because Hyginus says that, on campaign, a single century erected their tents in a row, eight men per tent, with the centurion's larger tent at the end (*De mun. castr.* 1). But the issue is not so clear cut. Hyginus allocates 100 tents to a *cohors milliaria*, ten of them for the centurions, which leaves the peculiar number of ninety tents to be distributed amongst the 10 *centuriae* (*De mun. castr.* 28). More worrying is his figure of 136 tents for a *cohors equitata milliaria*, minus 18 tents for the centurions and decurions (*De mun. castr.* 27); this presents an insoluble conundrum, unless we assume tent parties of different sizes. Finally, it is

The foundations of the *principia* at Aalen (Germany), exposed and consolidated for public view. The large fore-hall, spanning the line of the *via principalis*, is particularly striking. In the background is the Limesmuseum. (© Dietwulf Baatz)

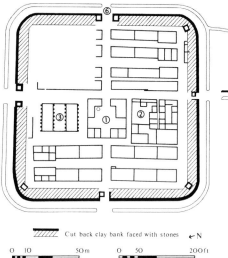

worth noting that, according to Vegetius, the basic squad, which he calls a *contubernium*, numbered ten men (Veg., *Epit.* 2.13). At any rate, however many men shared a barrack room, it follows logically that each type of unit, with differing numbers of *centuriae* and *turmae*, required different accommodation. But the correlation between fort and unit is not a simple one, as we shall see.

The sizes of auxiliary forts

Archaeology has revealed that Roman forts vary widely in size, from Rough Castle (Scotland) or Hesselbach (Germany), both measuring 0.6ha, to Newstead (Scotland) or Aalen (Germany), measuring respectively 5.9ha and six hectares. Many examples cluster around 1.2–1.4ha and 2–2.5ha.

Over 50 years ago, the late Professor Sir Ian Richmond suggested that the size of any given fort could be correlated with the particular type of auxiliary unit garrisoned there. In particular, he cited the 1.5ha Trajanic fort of Gelligaer (known to archaeologists as Gelligaer II; plan on p. 16) as the type-site for a standard infantry cohort (*cohors quingenaria*), on account of its six barrack blocks. However, the garrison of this fort remains unknown. Although Richmond's attribution is generally accepted, some have pointed out that the fort could equally have served a part-mounted cohort (*cohors equitata*), by accommodating its horsemen in the *retentura*, where there are two extra strip buildings.

For the larger milliary cohort, Richmond lighted upon the two-hectare fort of Housesteads (Roman Vercovicium), known to have been occupied by *cohors I Tungrorum milliaria*, and the morphologically similar, though somewhat smaller, 1.5ha fort of Fendoch (plan on p. 13). Although the garrison of Fendoch is unknown, both forts certainly have the ten barrack blocks expected for this type of unit (although there is an eleventh block at Housesteads).

Another possible candidate is the fort at Turnu Severin (Romania), Roman Drobeta (plan on p. 15), which may have housed a *cohors peditata milliaria*. At 1.7ha the fort falls squarely into the same size range as Fendoch and Housesteads, and the attested garrison, *cohors III Campestris c.R.*, seems to have been commanded by a tribune (CIL 3, 14216), which could indicate that it was milliary. But, although the fort appears to have had ten barrack blocks, each one has far fewer individual rooms than we would expect. To add further complication, the Trajanic building work was carried out by *cohors I Antiochensium* (AE 1959, 309), who may have shared the fort.

For the *cohors equitata*, Richmond preferred the two-hectare fort of Caerhun, known to the Romans as Kanovium (plan above). The ground plan could not be completely recovered, owing to the presence of a churchyard in the north-east quadrant. But if this area, the left *praetentura*, was a mirror image of the right, as is usually the case, there would have been six barrack blocks here, and a further two in the *retentura*, which would, in theory, provide the required accommodation for six centuries of infantry and four cavalry troops (although it now seems more likely that each *turma* required a complete barrack block to itself).

Künzing (Germany) in Raetia provides a more secure example of a *cohors equitata* fort (plan on p. 29). Later known to the Romans as Quintana, after the 3rd-century garrison, *cohors V (Quinta) Bracaraugustanorum*, the 2.3ha

Cut back clay bank faced with stones   ←N

0   10   50m   0   50   200ft

Plan of the fort at Caerhun. In the central range lie the *principia* (1), a large *praetorium* (2) and a pair of granaries, joined at each end (3). The bathhouse (4) lies some way to the east, outside the *porta praetoria* (6). A small annexe (5) has been tacked onto the south side. (© Author, after Hassall)

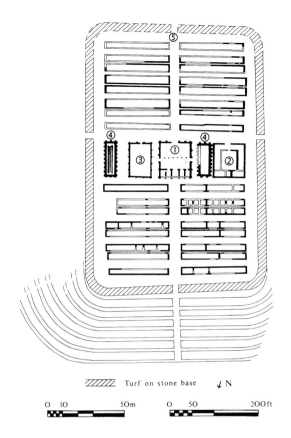

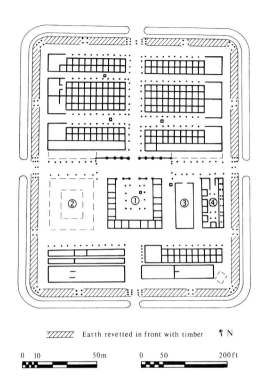

Turf on stone base ↙N

Earth revetted in front with timber ↑N

O 10   50m   O 50   200ft

0 10   50m   0 50   200ft

fort was originally built for *cohors III Thracum equitata*. However, it contains the odd number of nine barrack blocks, which presents a mystery. And Oberstimm (Germany) may also have housed a *cohors equitata* (plan on p. 9). Richmond's method of analysing area alone would place this 1.4ha fort in the size range for an infantry cohort, but the excavator found evidence of eight barrack blocks, which is surely too many for this type of unit. Unfortunately, not only is the fort's garrison unknown, but its plan also exhibits several peculiarities, which can be attributed to its Claudian date. But it is the 1.7ha fort at Wallsend (plan on p. 48) on Hadrian's Wall that presents the clearest case for a *cohors equitata* fort, with six infantry barracks and four cavalry barracks; the garrison is known to have been *cohors IV Lingonum equitata* (RIB 1299).

For the *cohors equitata milliaria*, Richmond selected the two-hectare fort of Birrens (Roman Blatobulgium; plan above left). Inscriptions attest the presence of *cohors I Nervana Germanorum milliaria equitata* there in the Antonine period. Excavations revealed 16 strip buildings in both the *praetentura* and the *retentura*, broadly arranged in pairs and probably to be interpreted, by and large, as barrack blocks. The internal arrangement of these buildings is unclear, and problems remain in deciding exactly where the unit's ten centuries and eight *turmae* were accommodated.

Richmond selected the forts of Chesters (Roman Cilurnum; plan on p. 17) and Benwell (Roman Condercum) on Hadrian's Wall as type-sites for the standard quingenary *ala*. Indeed, it now seems that the 2.3ha fort of Chesters was built for one of the three *alae Augustae* stationed in Britain, vindicating Richmond's theory. At Benwell, the *praetentura* was destroyed by a reservoir in the 19th century, so the fort's exact size is unknown, but it may have been similar to Chesters; although the original garrison is

ABOVE LEFT

Plan of the Antonine fort at Birrens. The central range comprises the usual *principia* (1), *praetorium* (2) and a pair of granaries (4). It is not clear why an extra double granary (3) was inserted. (© Author, after Hassall)

ABOVE RIGHT

Plan of the fort at Künzing. Eight barracks fill the *praetentura*. In the central range, the *principia* (1) is flanked by a granary (3) and store building (4). The site of the *praetorium* (2) is unexcavated. (© Author, after Hassall)

Comparative plans of Roman forts

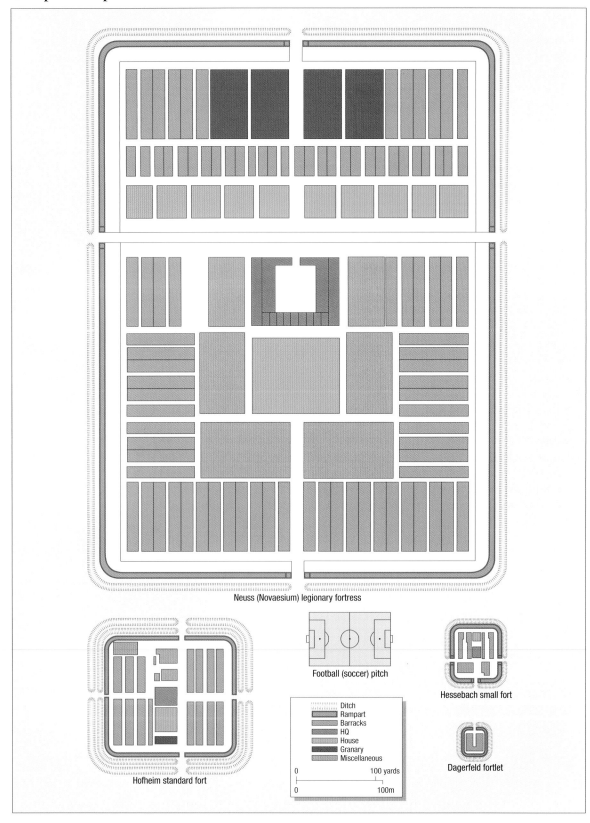

Neuss (Novaesium) legionary fortress

Hofheim standard fort

Football (soccer) pitch

Hessebach small fort

Dagerfeld fortlet

Ditch
Rampart
Barracks
HQ
House
Granary
Miscellaneous

0   100 yards
0   100m

unknown, the fort later housed *ala I Hispanorum Asturum*, and excavations revealed the kind of nine-roomed barrack block that, as we shall see (p. 49ff), may be characteristic of a cavalry garrison. In addition, the aggressive positioning of the fort, astride Hadrian's Wall with the three main gates lying to the north of the barrier, has suggested to some scholars that the garrison provided the kind of rapid response expected from a cavalry *ala*.

The milliary *ala* was the rarest of unit types, and any given provincial army would only have a single example. In Britain, this was *ala Augusta Gallorum Petriana*, stationed at Stanwix (Roman Uxelodunum) on Hadrian's Wall. Unfortunately, little is known of the internal arrangement of this four-hectare fort. The large size of Newstead (Roman Trimontium), and the 4.1ha fort at Dalswinton, suggested to Richmond and others that *ala Petriana* was stationed there in sequence, prior to its move to Stanwix; if so, it has left traces at neither site.

It is worth noting that the forts provided for this unit type elsewhere were considerably larger than these British examples. Under Domitian, *ala II Flavia milliaria* lay at Heidenheim (5.2ha) in the province of Raetia, before moving up to Aalen (6.1ha) in the mid-2nd century AD. However, we should be wary of using size alone to determine the identity of the intended occupants, as units could be divided or brigaded.

It is tempting to assume that the forts of Heddernheim (Frankfurt) and Niederbieber, which match Heidenheim in size, likewise held a milliary *ala*, and perhaps the same one in sequence; but no milliary *ala* was stationed in Upper Germany. In any case, the Vespasianic foundation of Heddernheim is rather early for this type of unit, which only appeared after around AD 80, and the unit in residence, *ala I Flavia gemina*, was a quingenary unit (e.g. CIL 13, 7365). Furthermore, the site has also produced gravestones of men from two different cohorts, *cohortes IV Vindelicorum* (e.g. CIL 13, 11947) and *XXXII voluntariorum civium Romanorum* (e.g. CIL 13, 7383); although they need not all have been there simultaneously, there is a possibility that a large fort like this one accommodated a composite garrison made up of elements from more than one unit. This seems to have been the case at Niederbieber, which was occupied by a pair of irregular units: *numerus exploratorum Germanicianorum Divitiensium* and a *numerus Brittonum*.

Aerial view of Hod Hill (Dorset, England). In the north corner, the defences of a Roman fort can be seen, utilizing the existing rampart as its north-east and north-west sides. (© Francesca M. Radcliffe)

Rear view of north gateway (*porta praetoria*) at Pfünz (Germany). It is thought that, in Roman times, the stonework was plastered over and painted white. (© Dietwulf Baatz)

It has also been suggested that a milliary *ala* could have occupied the 3.5ha fort of Slăveni (Romania) in the province of Dacia, although the garrison attested there, *ala I Hispanorum*, is not known to have been milliary. The fort is clearly much too large for any other single unit type, and the plan restored by the excavator would comfortably accommodate 24 *turmae*. But it seems that, like Niederbieber, the fort accommodated more than one unit, for the wonderfully named *ala I Claudia nova miscellanea* is also attested here, as well as *cohortes I Brittonum* and *I Flavia Commagenorum*.

The variation in fort plan, even between forts apparently intended for the same type of unit, should be taken as a lesson that the Romans did not slavishly follow some hypothetical blueprint. Equally, the difficulties should be obvious in attempting to assign units to forts, where unit identities are unknown and fort plans are incomplete. In any case, the entire practice is called into question by the Roman tendency to assign more than one unit to a single fort, as at Syene (Aswan, Egypt) which, in AD 118, accommodated three different *cohortes equitatae* (ILS 2483).

THE ELEMENTS OF AN AUXILIARY FORT

The overall layout of the fort: gates and roadways

Hyginus' *Liber de munitionibus castrorum*, although fragmentary, gives us a glimpse of the procedures used by Roman military surveyors. Strictly speaking, the text describes how to lay out the temporary camp of a large expeditionary army. But, when used with care, many details and much of the technical vocabulary can be transferred to the army's permanent fortifications.

The east gate (*porta principalis dextra*) at Künzing during excavation. The white poles indicate the positions of the original timber uprights. (© Dietwulf Baatz)

For example, Hyginus recommends that any camp should be *tertiata* ('in thirds'; *De mun. castr.* 21), which he illustrates with hypothetical dimensions of 2,400 x 1,600 feet (36ha), giving a 3:2 ratio. The resulting tertiate layout is best described as resembling a playing card, and (as we shall see) most Roman forts came to adopt this basic shape, before giving it up again in the later period. Hyginus believed that this shape was the best one to allow sufficient fresh air to circulate. Whether or not he was correct, ventilation and sanitation must have been major considerations in the siting of permanent forts. Although the earliest forts show a tendency to squareness, with a main thoroughfare dividing the interior into a front half and a rear half, there was a gradual move to a more rectangular plan, achieved by doubling the depth of the

Extra defences at Rough Castle on the Antonine Wall (Scotland) take the form of staggered rows of pits. Caesar used similar defences at the siege of Alesia, where he called them *lilia* ('lilies') as a macabre reference to the single sharpened stake concealed, like the stamen of a flower, in each pit. (© Author)

rear area. The effect of this was to create three distinct bands of buildings, which Hyginus calls the *praetentura* (the 'front'), the *retentura* (the 'back') and, in between, the *latera praetorii* (literally, the 'flanks of the commander's house'), because the commander was always situated in the middle of the camp.

By and large, every fort had four gateways (*portae*), one per side, although exceptions can be found. For example, the Claudio-Neronian fort at Valkenburg has no rear gate (plan on p. 8), and the special circumstances at Hod Hill, tucked in the corner of an earlier Iron Age hill fort where it utilized the native rampart as its north-east and north-west sides, meant that the builders could create only two gates. As the weak points on any defensive circuit, the gates were usually flanked by square or rectangular towers, while the entrance itself was bridged with a continuation of the rampart walkway, to allow the stationing of defenders there, should the need arise. Heavy wooden doors closed the portals. In a marching camp, the main entrance traditionally faced either east or towards the enemy (Hyg., *De mun. castr.* 56; Veg., *Epit.* 1.23), but we would expect more practical considerations to have governed the orientation of a permanent fort. Sometimes these considerations are elusive. For example, Heidenheim on the Upper German *limes* actually faces south, away from the frontier line. But other forts were perhaps oriented on nearby rivers; both Birrens and Heddernheim (Frankfurt) face south, so that their main gate (*porta praetoria*) opened onto the rivers Annan and Nidda, although enemy territory for both lay to the north.

The front of any fort is characterized by the T-shaped arrangement of roads which met at the centrally located headquarters building (*principia*). Standing at the door of the headquarters (*principia*), the fort commander had a clear view up the main street (*via praetoria*) to the main gate (*porta praetoria*). The *porta praetoria* was often the only double-portalled gateway into the fort; for this reason, it probably retained some ceremonial importance, and was often decorated with a commemorative inscription. From the same spot, looking to left and right, the fort commander had an unobstructed view along the fort's other main thoroughfare to each of the two side gates (*portae principales*). This lateral road was called the *via principalis* because it ran past the front of the *principia*.

In Hyginus' notional tertiate arrangement, the first of the three areas or bands within the fort was the *praetentura*. Stretching from the *via principalis*

Main gate (*porta praetoria*) of the Roman fort at Saalburg (Germany), showing one of the staircases for ascending the rampart. Key features of the fort, including the ramparts and gates, were reconstructed during the years 1899–1907. (© Author)

up to the front rampart, it was divided into two zones, to the left and to the right of the *via praetoria*. Both zones were normally filled with barrack buildings, laid out neatly in rows. The second band, the *latera praetorii*, comprised the row of buildings arranged on either side of the *principia*, fronting onto the *via principalis*. Archaeologists commonly refer to these buildings as the 'central range'. By and large, they consisted of the main administrative buildings. A minor roadway normally ran along the rear of the central range, parallel to the *via principalis*; in his marching camp, Hyginus calls this the *via quintana*. It was not normally linked to any gateways, except in very particular circumstances; for example, several forts project beyond Hadrian's Wall, so that their *portae principales* lie beyond the frontier wall, and in these cases *portae quintanae* were provided to allow full access from behind the frontier wall as well. Chesters provides a good example of this (plan on p. 17).

In the tertiate arrangement, the last of the three areas or bands was the *retentura*, which extended back from the *via quintana* to the fort's rear rampart. Like the *praetentura*, it was usually filled with barrack blocks. A rear gate (*porta decumana*) was normally located at the midpoint of the rear rampart, and from it the *via decumana* ran up to the back of the *principia*, dividing the *retentura* into two zones, one to the left and one to the right. Some larger forts had an exceptionally deep *retentura* (Fendoch is a good example: plan on p. 13), while in others it is hard to distinguish it from the central range (Oberstimm illustrates this: plan on p. 9). Furthermore, early forts had no *retentura* at all, consisting only of the *praetentura* and the *latera praetorii*, as at Valkenburg (plan on p. 8).

The communications network within the fort was completed by a perimeter road, the *via sagularis*, running along behind the rampart in the area that Hyginus calls the *intervallum*. Minor lanes were left between the buildings, corresponding to Hyginus' *viae vicenariae*, which gave access to the main roads from all parts of his camp (*De mun. castr.* 13, 14, 20).

The reconstructed west gateway at Welzheim-Ost (Germany). The wide embrasures gave soldiers on the ramparts maximum visibility. (© Dietwulf Baatz)

The defences

Forts were typically protected by a ditch system and defended by a rampart, which was either of stacked turves, giving the impression of a steep grassy banking, or a timber revetment retaining an earth core. From a base four to five metres wide, a height of three to 3.5m could be achieved. The sloping effect, either at the front and back or, in the case of the timber-revetted version, at the back only, resulted in a rampart-walk around two metres wide. The ramparts depicted on Trajan's Column appear to have been surfaced

Roman fort platform at Böhming (Germany) viewed from the air. Although a 16th-century churchyard occupies the site, excavations carried out in 1898 were able to locate the *principia* of this small fort. (© Andreas Thiel)

with a timber corduroy walkway, and provided with a timber breastwork at the front. This scheme was adopted for the reconstructed rampart at The Lunt (Baginton).

Such defences were perceived to be permanent, despite the organic nature of their materials, but they required constant maintenance. At a later stage, the turf banking was often cut back at the front and faced with a stone wall, and from the mid-1st century AD new forts were often built in stone from the outset. This was not a universal trend, as forts continued to be built using turf and timber. Equally, the rebuilding of earlier forts in stone was not prompted by some empire-wide policy of refurbishment, but proceeded piecemeal, as and when required. As late as AD 201, during the reign of Septimius Severus, the garrison of Bumbeşti (Romania) in the province of Dacia erected a pair of inscriptions announcing that, 'as the turf walls of the cohort's camp had fallen down because of old age' (*muros caespiticios castrorum cohortis … vetustate dilapsos*), the emperor and his sons 'restored them in stone' (*lapide eos restituerunt*: AE 1901, 46; ILS 9179).

Stone was not always readily available, and other durable building materials might be substituted. Visiting the fort of Phasis on the Black Sea coast around AD 132, the writer Arrian recorded that 'previously, the rampart was made of earth and the towers were of wood, but now the wall is constructed from baked bricks and the towers, too' (Arrian, *Peripl.* 9.4).

Where a stone wall was provided, it would have been carried up to form a parapet, perhaps 1.5m high and one metre thick; the remaining width, rather narrow for a functional wallwalk, would have been supplemented either by a timber-frame construction, or by the provision of an earthen banking at the rear. At the small 0.8ha fort of Wörth in the Odenwald, the collapse of complete sections of wall into the ditch has given archaeologists a unique insight into the

Remains of the north gate and rampart at Ellingen (Germany). Originally built in timber, the stone fort dates from AD 182. Unusually, it has only two gates. (© Dietwulf Baatz)

construction method. Here, built on top of a 0.7m deep foundation, the one-metre-thick wall consisted of a mortared rubble core faced by squared ashlar blocks, 32 courses at the front and more at the rear. It originally stood 4.15m up to the string course, above which sat the breastwork, 1.8m high and around 0.45m thick. The resulting walkway of 0.65m is far too narrow to be functional, so it must have been extended, perhaps by the addition of a timber construction; an earthen banking would surely have occupied far too much of the fort's already small internal area.

On the Antonine Wall in Scotland, the forts are predominantly of turf and timber construction, but two, Balmuildy and Castlecary, were constructed in stone. Their sturdy ramparts, firmly founded on a 2.7m-wide bed of clay-packed cobbles, stand comparison with Hadrian's Wall in size and quality. At Castlecary in particular, the builders artfully stepped the rampart in, from a bottom course 2.4m wide and a second course 2.1m wide to a third course of chamfered blocks, reducing the wall to its final width of two metres. The provision of a crenellated breastwork would still leave ample space for a walkway; but, even so, it has been suggested that the wall was backed with an earthen banking.

Towers originally flanked the four gateways; others were positioned at the four corners as well, and often in the interval between gate and corner. In the timber variety, the lower storey of the gate towers was probably boarded in to provide guard chambers, but elsewhere the towers would have consisted of four massive corner posts, supporting a platform some way above the rampart. The evidence of Trajan's Column suggests that the upper levels of towers were left open, perhaps to reduce wind resistance; it is not certain whether or not they were roofed, although this would have been advisable in northern Europe. Of course, rebuilding in stone would have afforded the opportunity of roofing any previously unroofed towers.

Fort building is depicted on Trajan's Column as a task for legionaries (e.g. scene 32, Cast XII; scenes 344–45, Cast CXXVII), and it is usually pointed out that it was legionary work-gangs who built Hadrian's Wall and the Antonine Wall. Inscriptions provide further evidence. For example, in AD 181, at the fort of Böhming (Germany) on the Raetian frontier, a vexillation of *legio III Italica* built the rampart, including the gates and towers (AE 1899, 195: *vexillarii legionis III Italicae vallum fecerunt … item portas cum turribus*).

Site of the *principia* at Bar Hill on the Antonine Wall (Scotland). The foundations have been consolidated and marked out with concrete. The well in the foreground is a standard feature of this type of building. Behind it is the wall of the *basilica*, and beyond lies the row of rooms flanking the *aedes*. (© Author)

The central range and *retentura* of the Raetian fort at Weißenburg (Germany). The consolidated foundations of the *principia* can clearly be seen, with its fore-hall spanning the *via principalis*. To its right lie the commander's house (*praetorium*) and a granary. (© Dietwulf Baatz)

However, there is plenty of evidence that auxiliaries could be employed in building their own forts. It is possible that technical specialists such as surveyors and engineers were borrowed from the legions, but the construction work itself was surely not beyond the expertise of the *auxilia*. During the reign of Hadrian, the specialist archers of *cohors I Hamiorum* were engaged in building their fort at Carvoran; two work gangs even specified that they each 'walled [the fort] for 112 feet' (*vallavit pedes CXII*: RIB 1818, 1820).

Elsewhere, auxiliaries are found repairing their fortifications. For example, at Risingham, a beautifully crafted circular inscription records that, in around AD 205, the garrison rebuilt a gate and its walls from the ground up, because it had fallen down through old age (*portam cum muris vetustate dilapsis … cohors I Vangionum milliaria equitata … a solo restituit*: RIB 1234). Similarly, *cohors IV Gallorum*, stationed at Vindolanda in the AD 220s, proudly announced that they had restored a gateway and its towers from the foundations (*portam cum turribus a fundamentis restituerunt*: RIB 1706), while at roughly the same time *cohors II Treverorum equitata* were rebuilding the wall of their fort at Zugmantel 'from the ground up' (*murum a solo fecit*: CIL 13, 7612). And, although the inscriptions from Bumbeşti (above) do not explicitly say so, the work was surely carried out by the named unit, *cohors I Aurelia Brittonum milliaria*. Unusually, in AD 182, at the fort of Ellingen in Raetia, 'the wall and gates of castellum Sablonetum were replaced in stone' by the provincial governor's infantry guardsmen (*kastelli Sabloneti murum cum portis lapidibus substitutum … per singulares pedites*: AE 1983, 730); but these guards were, in any case, drawn from the province's auxiliary garrison.

The headquarters building

The headquarters building (*principia*) was the focus of each fort, located in the middle of the central range. Designed as a scaled-down version of its legionary counterpart, it comprised a paved courtyard, often surrounded by colonnaded walkways, and a rear range of rooms flanking a central shrine (*aedes*) and often fronted by a long cross-hall (*basilica*). The correct terminology is provided by an inscription from Reculver (England), which mentions the *aedes principiorum cum basilica* (AE 1962, 258).

A standard fixture of the courtyard appears to have been a well, perhaps to ensure that there was one secure water source in the fort. Indeed, it was the well in the headquarters at Rough Castle, on the Antonine Wall, that

Central range at Pen Llystyn fort, c. AD 80

Discovered and excavated in the 1950s, the fort of Pen Llystyn was occupied for around a decade during the Flavian period. An annexe lay in front of the fort, but the bathhouse was never located. The site has now been almost completely destroyed by gravel extraction. A complete ground plan was recovered, demonstrating the standard arrangement of barracks and central range buildings. A large and well-appointed *praetorium* lay to one side of the *principia*, while the usual pair of granaries lay to the other, where they were accessible to wagons entering by the *porta principalis*.

produced proof of the building's correct name. For a long time, it was assumed that the headquarters building in any Roman fort was officially designated as the *praetorium*, but the excavations in 1903 produced epigraphic evidence to the contrary: an inscription which had been tossed into the well during the evacuation of the fort around AD 160 clearly recorded the fact that 'the Sixth Cohort of Nervians built the *principia*' (*cohors VI Nerviorum principia fecit*: RIB 2145).

A building inscription from Lanchester (England) specifies that the garrison 'restored the derelict headquarters building and armoury' (*principia et armamentaria conlapsa restituit*: RIB 1092). This seems to imply that the armoury was part of the headquarters building, reflecting the situation in the larger legionary *principia*, where rows of rooms flanking the courtyard served this purpose. Of course, there may have been a separate armoury store (*armamentarium*) in many forts, particularly those like Aalen where the *principia* courtyard lacked even colonnades, far less rooms. A separate building is certainly implied by an inscription from Roomburg, which records the rebuilding of an 'armoury that had fallen down through old age' (*armamentarium vetustate conlabsum*: ILS 9178). However, a quantity of weapons and military equipment

The *principia* at Housesteads on Hadrian's Wall (England). On the right is the row of rooms invariably found at the rear of the headquarters. On the left is the cross-hall (*basilica*) with column bases *in situ* and, in the middle of the far wall, the entrance from the courtyard can be seen. (© Author)

came to light in the *principia* at Niederbieber, and other forts have produced similar evidence. For example, the well-known 3rd-century hoard of cavalry parade equipment from Künzing was discovered in the *principia*. Wherever it was stored, military equipment (*armamenta*) was in the care of a *custos armorum*, a functionary routinely attested in the legions, but who existed in many auxiliary units, too (e.g. *ala Frontiniana* in Pannonia inferior: CIL 3, 3400; *cohors I Vindelicorum* in Dacia: AE 1977, 697; *cohors I Aelia sagittaria* in Noricum: AE 1992, 1440).

The *principia* often incorporated a *basilica* running the full width of the courtyard. Here the fort commander would have discharged his various official and judicial duties, and presided over religious observances. The *basilica* usually has a raised dais (*tribunal*) at one end, where the commander would take his place. A remarkable inscription from the fort at Remagen (Germany) records how, in AD 218, the commander 'repaired the clock at his own expense because it did not show the hours correctly and was worn out with old age' (*horolegium ab horis intermissum et vetustate conlabsum suis inpendiis restituit*: ILS 9363). The watches of the day and night were probably announced from the *principia*, so a clock of some sort would be essential.

Behind the *basilica* ran a series of rooms, often five in number, of which the central one was the shrine (*aedes*) where the unit's sacred standards (*signa*) were kept. On account of this, the building clearly had religious overtones, as shown by the frequent finds of altars during their excavation. An inscription from Aalen, dedicated to Septimius Severus and his sons, records the restoration of the 'derelict *capitolium* and *principia*' by the garrison in AD 208 (AE 2001, 1566: *ala II Flavia milliaria pia fidelis capitolium cum principiis vetustate conlapsis restituit*); the term *capitolium* is an unusual one, normally indicating a temple of Jupiter, but probably indicates the *aedes*. Certainly, the so-called Feriale Duranum, a calendar of religious observances discovered in the archive of *cohors XX Palmyrenorum* at Dura Europus, frequently lists sacrifices by the unit to Jupiter and the Capitoline gods. The maintenance of the Aalen *principia* had clearly been neglected during the 45 years since its construction under Marcus Aurelius (AE 1986, 528).

The standard bearers (*signiferi*) of the Roman Army had financial responsibilities, too (Veg., *Epit*. 2.20). Consequently, in many forts, a strongroom (possibly known as the *aerarium*) was created beneath the floor of the *aedes*, either by elevating the room (as at South Shields) or by digging a basement (as at Vindolanda) to safeguard the official funds and the soldiers' savings; often the unit's pay chest was simply kept in a pit under the floor (as at Oberstimm). The other rooms were perhaps offices (*tabularia*) occupied by various clerks, processing the mountain of documentation that each unit

Reconstructed granary at The Lunt Roman fort, Baginton (England). There is a covered loading bay at each end and sufficient room for wagons to unload. (© The Lunt Roman Fort / Coventry Heritage and Arts Trust Ltd)

generated. The papyri records of the cohort at Dura Europus show that men were routinely assigned to the commander's *officium* (staff), probably carrying out duties similar to the copyist (*librarius*) of the *numerus Brittonum* at Niederbieber, who set up an altar to the 'Spirit of the Records Office' (*Genius tabularii*: CIL 13, 7752). In later forts, some of these rooms received under-floor heating, perhaps to preserve the archives or to make life more amenable for the clerks.

In many forts, mostly along the German and Raetian frontier (e.g. Aalen and Zugmantel) but also at Newstead and Wallsend, the *principia* was fronted by a forehall, projecting across the *via principalis*. In each case, the *principia* lacked a cross-hall, so the forehall perhaps fulfilled the function of the missing *basilica*. However, some scholars have interpreted it as the cavalry drill hall mentioned by Vegetius (*porticus equestris*: *Epit.* 2.23). An inscription set up in the fort at Netherby (England) for the emperor Severus Alexander proclaims that *cohors I Hispanorum milliaria equitata* 'have now built and completed a cavalry exercise hall, begun long ago, from the ground up' (*baselicam equestrem exercitatoriam iam pridem a solo coeptam aedificavit consummavitque*: RIB 978). Unfortunately, the fort's *principia* remains inaccessible beneath the stately home of Netherby Hall, so it is impossible to check whether it had a forehall instead of a cross-hall.

Excavations in the left *praetentura* of the fort at Valkenburg revealed the remains of a timber granary. The characteristic ground plan can be seen, with parallel timber sleepers supporting the heavy floor while allowing air to circulate underneath. (© Provinzie Zuid Holland)

Granaries

Besides accommodation for the officers and men, the only other buildings regularly found in forts are the food storage buildings, or 'granaries' (*horrea*), which reportedly held rations for a year (Tac., *Agr.* 22) or for even longer (as at Premnis, above p. 9). These buildings, often built in pairs, have a distinctive ground plan for two reasons. First, in both timber and stone-built granaries, the floor was raised. The external walls had ground-level ventilation gaps to allow air to circulate freely beneath the building, and the wooden planked (or occasionally stone-flagged) floor was underpinned either by multiple parallel sleeper walls (e.g. Fendoch, plan on p. 13), or by several longitudinal dwarf walls (e.g. Birrens, plan on p. 29), or by a checkerboard pattern of short pillars (e.g. Niederbieber; Housesteads). Second, in stone-built examples, the walls were externally buttressed, perhaps to offset the effect of these ventilation gaps, or perhaps simply to carry the roof well beyond the walls in order to keep the eaves-drip clear of the foundations. Of course, when building in stone, the opportunity was perhaps taken to heighten the building, creating additional storage space.

Building identified as a hospital (*valetudinarium*) at the Hadrian's Wall fort of Housesteads (England). (© Author)

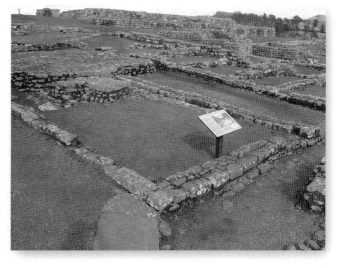

Principia fore-hall at Saalburg (Germany). This feature of the *principia* is rarely found outside Germany, but seems to be the equivalent of the *basilica principiorum*, or cross-hall, found elsewhere. (© Andreas Thiel)

Attempts have periodically been made to correlate granary floor space with size of garrison. However, there are too many imponderables for the conclusions to be anything more than possibilities. Besides the obvious difficulty in divining the actual garrison of any given fort, with units routinely divided or brigaded together, we have no idea how foodstuffs were stored in the *horreum*. Some have suggested that timber bins or hoppers lined the walls, to carry the loose grain that was the soldiers' staple ration. But such grain would have been more easily handled in sacks, and other foodstuffs were probably stored in the same building. Besides the cereal that was normally baked into bread, soldiers received a ration of salt, and oil or lard. And the Celtic beer at Vindolanda (*cervesa*: *Tab. Vindol.* 2, 158; 190) perhaps required storage in the granary.

The garrison of Niederbieber dedicated a statue of the 'Spirit of the Granaries' (*Genio horreorum numeri Brittonum Antoninianorum*: CIL 13, 7749), no doubt to safeguard these important buildings. But, in some forts, even the granaries seem to have been neglected. At Great Chesters on Hadrian's Wall, an inscription proudly advertises the fact that 'the soldiers of *cohors II Asturum* completely rebuilt the granary, which had fallen down through old age' (*horreum vetustate conlabsum milites cohortis II Asturum … a solo restituerunt*: RIB 1738). *Cohors I Aelia Dacorum* at Birdoswald even built their own granary, with assistance from men of another cohort (*horreum fecerunt cohortes I Aelia Dacorum et I Thracum civium Romanorum*: RIB 1909).

Hospitals

It is well known that the legions, with their larger pool of specialists, routinely incorporated a hospital (*valetudinarium*) within their fortresses, staffed by medical officers (*medici*) and orderlies, and run by an *optio valetudinarii*. It would have been beyond the means of most auxiliary units to maintain the same level of service, but some larger forts appear to have had hospital buildings and medical staff. One of the well-known Vindolanda tablets mentions a hospital, perhaps in the process of construction, as the tablet records the assignment of men to various building tasks (*Tab. Vindol.* 2, 155). Another tablet lists men sent 'with Marcus the medical officer', not to practice medicine, but rather oddly to build some sort of residence (*ad hospitium faciendum cum Marco medico*: *Tab. Vindol.* 2, 156). At Beroea (Halab, Syria), *cohors IV Lucensium* set up an inscription declaring that 'a hospital has been built from scratch' (*valetudinarium a novo factum*: AE 1987, 952). And in AD 179, *cohors II Aurelia nova equitata* recorded the building of a hospital at Stojnik near Belgrade (Serbia) in the province of Moesia Superior (ILS 9174).

Military hospitals are thought to have taken the form of a central courtyard, surrounded by individual rooms, like the legionary hospitals in miniature. Such buildings have been identified at Wallsend and at Housesteads, where the tombstone of a 25-year-old doctor was found (RIB 1618). Conclusive proof is lacking, but both buildings incorporated a system of running water and a latrine in the south-west corner, both of which were necessary features of a hospital. However, neither site has produced the kind of medical instruments known from Saalburg and Zugmantel.

Besides combat wounds and the general run of illnesses that afflict those living in close proximity to one another, eye disorders are thought to have been particularly prevalent in the military. One of the Vindolanda tablets, a strength report from around AD 95, lists '15 men sick, six wounded, and ten suffering from eye inflammation' (*aegri xv, volnerati vi, lippientes x*: *Tab. Vindol.* 2, 154). It is unclear whether such casualties were hospitalized, or simply confined to barracks.

North granary at Housesteads, showing the heavily buttressed outer wall and the rows of little pillars which once supported a raised floor. (© Author)

View from the reconstructed rampart at The Lunt Roman fort. The reconstruction of the *gyrus* can be seen in the background. (© The Lunt Roman Fort / Coventry Heritage and Arts Trust Ltd)

Medical officers (*medici*) are known from several forts in Upper Germany, which may imply the presence of hospitals there. Inscriptions were set up at Osterburken by the *medicus* of *cohors III Aquitanorum* (CIL 13, 11767) and at Groß-Krotzenburg by the *medicus* of *cohors IV Vindelicorum* (CIL 13, 7415), while Marcus Rubrius Zosimus, *cohors IV Aquitanorum*'s doctor at Obernburg, set up a dedication to Jupiter and a selection of the gods of his profession: Apollo, Aesculapius, Salus and Fortuna (CIL 13, 6621).

The doctor at Niederbieber, who (like Anicius Ingenuus from Housesteads) emphasized that he was a *medicus ordinarius*, set up a dedication to the 'Spirit of the Wound-dressers' (*Genius capsariorum*: ILS 9182) from his own savings. As a *medicus ordinarius*, he is likely to have been a high-ranking officer on a par with a centurion. The 'wound-dressers' (*capsarii*), on the other hand, were ordinary soldiers who were excused general fatigues in return for practising their speciality (*immunes*).

Other buildings

The investigation of Roman forts usually turns up various nondescript buildings for which no particular function can be identified. Many of these will have been store buildings of some kind. The *ballistarium* mentioned in two inscriptions from High Rochester was long supposed to have been some sort of platform for mounting artillery, but it is more likely to have been a store building to protect the *ballistae* from the damp British weather. *Cohors I fida Vardullorum* first built the structure in AD 220 (*ballistarium a solo … fecit*: RIB 1280) and, 15 or so years later, commemorated its repair (*ballistarium a solo restituit*: RIB 1281).

Another so-far unique building is the so-called *gyrus* at The Lunt. This circular arena, 34m in diameter, with an artificially levelled interior, is thought to have been a training ground for horses. The fort's east rampart was remodelled in order to make room for it.

The annexe of the Antonine Wall fort at Rough Castle (Scotland) probably contained workshops as well as the bathhouse. The rampart marking out the annexe can be seen through the trees as a raised mound. (© Author)

Fort annexes

Many Roman forts had a defended annexe, which appears as an area tacked onto one side of the main fort and varies in size from site to site. The annexe was always a secondary feature, as demonstrated by the fact that the fort's main ditch system usually intervenes, creating a clear zone of separation. Annexes are most obvious along the Antonine Wall, where it was assumed that these supplementary enclosures were intended to replace the continuous military zone that snakes along the rear of Hadrian's Wall. However, although the often-ephemeral traces of an annexe are easily overlooked, the phenomenon is fairly widespread. Annexes were perhaps the precursors of the military villages (*vici*) that grew up around many forts.

The presence of an annexe has usually been detected by aerial photography, as archaeologists have traditionally concentrated on the main fort; consequently, few have been investigated even cursorily. Nevertheless, it is clear from examples along the Antonine Wall in particular that there was often a concentration of open-ended timber strip-buildings, interpreted as the sort of workshops (*fabricae*) that could accommodate a variety of activities. Inside forts, courtyard or corridor buildings are often interpreted as workshops (e.g., building four at Künzing; plan on p. 29), but noisy and often smelly manufacturing activities were better restricted to an annexe.

The discovery, in various different annexes, of slag for iron-smelting, lead ingots and scraps of copper alloy, along with the remains of furnaces, smithing hearths and stone moulds, indicates the kind of industrial processes that might have been hazardous and disagreeable if conducted within the confines of the main fort. One of the Vindolanda tablets appears to be a list of workmen (*Tab. Vindol.* 2, 160) who had perhaps been granted immunity from general fatigues on account of their speciality. The list of these specialists (*immunes*), drawn up by the Antonine military jurist Taruttienus Paternus (*Digest* 50.6.7), is often assumed to apply only to the legions. But the soldiers from the Vindolanda garrison who were assigned 'to the kilns' (*ad furnaces*: *Tab. Vindol.* 2, 155) may have been involved in weapons manufacture, perhaps as 'coppersmiths' (*aerarii*) and 'blacksmiths' (*ferrarii*).

Of course, metalworking alone could not satisfy the army's many requirements. There must have been a constant demand for organic materials, as well. The army utilized various items of wood, bone, leather and textile, whose manufacture (often incorporating unpleasant processes, especially in the case of leather working) would have been best confined to the annexe. Besides the frequent finds of leather items preserved in the damp, anaerobic environment of Vindolanda, one of the writing tablets from that site reveals the fact that hides were being received from the fort at Catterick, where they were evidently processed in bulk. There is also mention of a large quantity of sinew in the same writing tablet (*Tab. Vindol.* 2, 343). And, of the 343 men assigned to the Vindolanda *fabricae* on one particular day, 12 were 'leather workers' (*sutores*: *Tab. Vindol.* 2, 155). Taruttienus Paternus' list includes 'wagon makers' (*carpentarii*), and it is interesting to note that another of the Vindolanda tablets is a letter confirming the dispatch of a consignment of wagon components (*Tab. Vindol.* 2, 309):

Roofing tiles from Schirenhof (Schwäbisch Gmünd, Germany). Many Roman units manufactured tiles for their own use and for other units that lacked tile-making facilities. They generally stamped an abbreviation of their official title on each tile. These ones read CORPRET, which probably stands for *cohors Prima Raetorum.* (© Jona Lendering)

modiola numero xxxiiii	hubs, 34 in number
axses carrarios numero xxxiix	axles for carts, 38 in number
inibi axsis tornatus numero i	amongst these, a lathe-turned axle
radia numero ccc	spokes, 300 in number
sessiones numero viii	seats, eight in number
plutea numero xx[…]	wicker panels, 20+ in number

The everyday pottery items used in forts were normally imported from specialist centres, but some forts operated tile-making kilns. One such is known at Groß-Krotzenburg (Germany), where the garrison produced roofing tiles stamped with their name: 'COHIIIIVIND', as shorthand for *cohors IV Vindelicorum*. Their tiles were used as far afield as Niederbieber, where the garrison presumably lacked their own tile kilns.

LIVING IN A ROMAN FORT

The commander's house (*praetorium*)

Each auxiliary unit was commanded by an officer drawn from the equestrian aristocracy. Such men were second only to the senatorial order in terms of wealth, and were socially far superior to the ordinary soldiers, who normally were not even Roman citizens. During the early empire, a progression of military posts, the so-called *tres militiae* ('three military commands'), evolved for the sons of equestrian families, as part of their municipal career. The first step was as *praefectus cohortis*, prefect of an infantry or equitate cohort, after which a man could progress to a tribunate, either in a legion as *tribunus angusticlavius* ('narrow-stripe tribune', indicating his equestrian origin) or in command of a milliary cohort. The few cohorts of citizens, denoted by the additional title *civium Romanorum*, seem also to have been commanded by tribunes, as a special mark of respect. For those men who wished to continue their military career, the third step was as *praefectus alae*, prefect of a cavalry unit. A fourth step was added, probably under Domitian, when the introduction of a few milliary *alae* required suitably experienced commanders.

The fort commander was housed in generous quarters, as befitted his status as a middle-ranking equestrian. He was often accompanied on his tour of duty by his family and a retinue of slaves. For example, Flavius Cerialis, who commanded *cohors IX Batavorum* at Vindolanda around AD 100, was accompanied by his wife, Sulpicia Lepidina, and their family; the excavation of the Vindolanda *praetorium* famously produced many shoes which belonged to women and children, as well as a single tiny sock. The Vindolanda tablets tell us that the *praetorium* at one of the neighbouring forts was occupied by Aelius Brocchus, his wife Claudia Severa, and their little son (the *filiolus* mentioned in *Tab. Vindol.* 2,291). More poignant evidence comes from Birdoswald on Hadrian's Wall, where the commander, Aurelius Julianus, set up a tombstone commemorating his infant son 'who lived for one year and five days' (*vixit annum unum dies V*: RIB 1919).

In Hyginus' marching camp, the commander's tent was located in the centre. The same layout was retained in the fort, where the *praetorium* was invariably sited in the central range beside (or, very occasionally, behind) the *principia*. And, as a small reminder of civilization, the *praetorium* followed the plan of a luxurious Roman town house, the so-called *peristyle* form. Basically, four ranges of rooms surrounded a colonnaded courtyard, or *peristylium*, which was probably laid out as a garden. Other rooms could be added on to the side, as at Chesters and Mumrills, where a baths suite occupied respectively the east and south wing. The inward-looking design of the house preserved the commander's privacy by presenting blank facades to those on the outside.

Besides living rooms and a garden for the family's use, the *praetorium* had to have servants' quarters and a kitchen. The Vindolanda tablets give us a glimpse of the range and variety of foodstuffs that the commander's household consumed: pork and venison, apples and plums, ham and eggs. The commander also required public rooms, where he could meet and entertain his fellow officers. It seems that Brocchus was a dinner guest at Vindolanda on more than one occasion, and the famous birthday invitation (*Tab. Vindol.* 2,291) shows that Brocchus' wife could be expected to entertain her own friends, as well.

One of the barrack blocks at Chesters on Hadrian's Wall (England), partially exposed and consolidated. The officer's block can be seen projecting from the end. The drain runs along the middle of the lane separating two facing barrack blocks. (© Author)

We have seen that the Roman military took a pride in their work, by setting up dedicatory inscriptions whenever some major construction was completed. Flavius Neon, the fort commander at Volubilis in Mauretania Caesariensis, generously proclaimed that, 'by the labour of his fellow-soldiers, he designed and built the *praetorium* from scratch' (*praetorium per manus commilitum a solo composuit et fecit*: ILS 9175). Other inscriptions could be brutally honest. One example from Birdoswald records the rebuilding, at some point during the years AD 297–305, of the *praetorium* 'which was covered in earth and had fallen into ruin' (*quod erat humo copertum et in labem conlapsum*: RIB 1912). Presumably it had deteriorated through neglect, but it is not clear where the commander had been living in the meantime.

The barrack blocks

As in the legionary fortresses, so in the smaller forts, the most numerous building was the barrack block. This was a long, narrow building which, for about three-quarters of its length, comprised a row of double rooms, fronted by a continuous veranda; each pair of rooms consisted of a smaller, outer room, entered from the veranda, and a larger, inner room. For the remainder of its length, the building followed a different design, in which several rooms were arranged as a suite.

Soldiers often referred to one another as *contubernalis* ('room mate'), presumably referring to the fact that they were accommodated together in the same 'hut' (*taberna*) or barrack room. For example, in one of the Vindolanda tablets, the writer urges the recipient to 'greet Elpis, [illegible name], Rhenus, Tetricus and all your room-mates' (*saluta Elpidem … Rhenum Tetricum et omnes contibernales*: Tab. Vindol. 2,346). There is an obvious relationship with the word *contubernium*, which Vegetius uses for a squad of soldiers. And indeed, a sherd of a *mortarium* (mixing bowl) discovered at Usk (Wales) had been scratched with the inscription 'mixing bowl belonging to Messor's *contubernium*' (*pelveis contubernio Miissoris*: AE 1976, 370), corroborating the idea that certain equipment was held communally.

When in the field, each squad of men occupied their own tent. And indeed, the design of the barrack blocks found in Roman forts seems to be influenced by the arrangement of the tents in a temporary camp (see above, p. 27): the larger rear room can be equated with the tent itself (*papilio*), while the smaller front room logically represents the space for stacking each tent party's equipment (*armamenta*). Consequently, archaeologists sometimes refer to each double room as a *contubernium*, implying that it accommodated a squad of soldiers. Finally, the separate complex of rooms

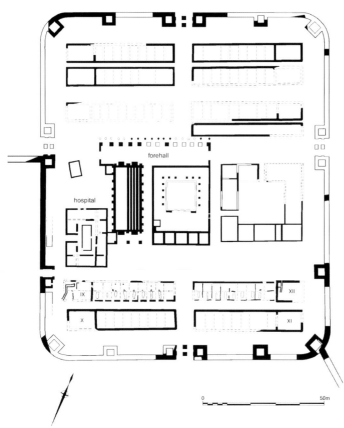

Plan of the fort at Wallsend, showing the cavalry barracks in the *retentura*. It is unusual for the *principia* of a fort in Britain to have a fore-hall. (© Tyne and Wear Museums)

forehall

hospital

IX

X

XI

XII

0   50m

at the end of the barrack matches the large campaign tent of the centurion, whose elevated status guaranteed him more spacious quarters.

In forts, the barrack blocks are often grouped in pairs, facing one another across an alleyway. If each barrack accommodated a single century, and the soldiers were distributed eight men per double room, then the barrack ought to have ten pairs of rooms. And if, for example, a *cohors peditata milliaria* had ten centuries, then its fort required ten barrack blocks. This was exactly how the archaeologist Sir Ian Richmond reconstructed the remains that he excavated at Fendoch (plan on p. 13). However, archaeological evidence from other sites suggests that this interpretation may be too simplistic.

Modern excavations at South Shields and Vindolanda have shed more light on the design of infantry barracks. In every case, the width of the front room was reduced by the insertion of a one-metre-wide corridor, running from the veranda past the front room, directly into the rear room. A similar layout was observed in the barracks at Lorch, on the outer *limes* of Upper Germany where it borders with Raetia. Although the rear room was invariably provided with a hearth, confirming its use as a living space, the front room occasionally had a hearth, as well. It is not yet clear whether this means that both rooms accommodated men, or whether perhaps the front room might have been reserved for cooking and eating. It is worth noting that no fort had a building specially reserved for the communal cooking and taking of meals, and it has always been assumed that men ate in their barracks.

It is convenient to continue thinking that, in infantry barracks, each double room accommodated a *contubernium*. However, although many fort barracks have ten double rooms, there are anomalies like Drobeta, with only four or five (plan on p. 15). Mounted units clearly presented a different problem, since cavalrymen were assigned, not to centuries of 80 men, but to troops of around 30 men. The solution seemed to be the allocation of two *turmae* per barrack block, and the provision of separate stable buildings for their mounts. However, modern research at Wallsend and South Shields has demonstrated a different scenario. Careful excavation of the barracks revealed the presence of an elongated urine pit in each of the front rooms, stone-lined and covered with a slab, while the rear room contained a hearth located against the party wall. Such pits had already been identified in buildings within the cavalry fort at Dormagen (Germany), where chemical analysis proved the presence of horse urine, but there was an initial reluctance to recognize the buildings as barracks, preferring to see them as stables. The British findings make the identification as barracks certain, and the consequences are clear: Roman cavalrymen routinely shared accommodation with their mounts. This can be seen to make perfect sense, as the rider was on hand to tend to his mount and deploy rapidly, whenever required.

It has been calculated that, in such a cavalry barrack, three horses could share the front room, leaving the rear room for their three riders. In this way, the nine double-rooms in the barracks at Wallsend and South Shields could accommodate a *turma* of 27 men, with three officers in the end suite making up a total of 30. Similar nine-roomed barracks are known at Benwell, so this was perhaps a recognized scheme for a cavalry garrison.

In the later period, it used to be thought that the standard barrack blocks of the 1st and 2nd centuries AD were replaced by rows of five or six detached chalets, whose crude construction reflected the declining standards of the military; they were separated, it seemed, to accommodate a family unit in place of each *contubernium*. Evidence from the 19th-century excavations at High Rochester

E

Excavations in 1997–98 at the fort of Wallsend on Hadrian's Wall revealed the barrack blocks occupied by the cavalry element of a *cohors equitata*. These exhibited the usual division of accommodation into units, sometimes called *contubernia*, each comprising a front room and a rear room. But each block had only nine of these units, plus a more spacious end suite, presumably for the officers. Archaeologists made the surprising discovery that the troopers shared their accommodation with their mounts, as demonstrated by the provision of large urine pits in the front rooms. It seems that one entire block accommodated a single *turma*.

and Housesteads gave rise to the theory. However, modern excavations at Vindolanda and South Shields have shown that this interpretation was mistaken. At both sites, the 3rd-century barracks were constructed to a high standard, although they were now shorter, comprising only five or six double rooms, in addition to the officer's quarters. But there are surely implications for the size of the century, which must have had a reduced complement, at these forts at least.

Women in the fort?

It is well known that soldiers were forbidden to marry. The historian Cassius Dio explains that 'since the men serving in the army could not legally have wives, they were granted the privileges of married men' by the emperor Claudius (Cass. Dio 60.24.3). This ban remained in force for two centuries until Septimius Severus 'granted the soldiers many privileges they had not previously enjoyed'; in particular, he allowed them 'to live with their wives' (Herodian 3.8.4–5). But, of course, during all that time, soldiers continued to make liaisons with local women, although any offspring remained illegitimate until their father's honourable discharge conferred *conubium* ('the right of legal marriage') and citizenship.

It has usually been assumed that the fort ramparts constituted a barrier between military and civilian. And, furthermore, although soldiers were at liberty to act in the civilian sphere, civilians would have had rather more restricted access to the military area. Some scholars claim to have found

Roman bathhouse at Bearsden on the Antonine Wall (Scotland). The remains have been consolidated for visitors. In the foreground, the flue from the furnace can be seen, serving the hottest room of the suite (*caldarium*). Behind, the rooms are progressively cooler, finally reaching the changing room (marked out by timber posts) and the building's entrance. (© Author)

evidence of women and children in Roman forts, through the identification of allegedly female artefacts (including infant burials in a barrack at South Shields as a proxy indicator). In fact, the evidence is rather thin. Hair pins from a 4th-century barrack block at South Shields are an ambiguous witness, and the women's shoes from Vindolanda, often cited in this regard, clearly belonged to the commander's family.

The bathhouse (*balneum*)

Most forts were provided with a bathhouse for the use of the troops. Only rarely are these buildings found within the ramparts, and it may have been the increased fire risk that caused them to be sited extramurally. Equally, there may have been a desire to separate military routine from the leisured atmosphere of the baths. In order to incorporate a hypocaust system, not just under the floor but in the wall cavities as well, bathhouses were generally built of masonry, even when associated with a turf-and-timber fort. This will have had the additional benefit of preventing deterioration from dampness and maintaining constant temperatures in the various rooms. But the entrance hall and dressing room, lacking the necessity for central heating, were often added in timber.

Two distinctive layouts are found. The *Reihentyp* (a German classification meaning 'row-type') is where the changing room (*apodyterium*), cold room (*frigidarium*), warm room (*tepidarium*) and hot room (*caldarium*) are arranged in a simple linear sequence. A good example of this type can be seen at the Antonine Wall fort of Bearsden (Scotland). A more sophisticated *Blocktyp* ('block-type') clustering of rooms is also found, for example at Chesters on Hadrian's Wall (England). Both types often incorporated a specialized dry-heat room (*sudatorium* or *laconicum*). The general design and ordering of rooms reflect the Romans' customary bathing process. This was basically a sequence of three stages: the bather moved from the *frigidarium*, an unheated room that usually incorporated one or more cold water plunge pools, to the *tepidarium*, which was moderately heated; he then moved on to the *caldarium* (hot room), which often incorporated a hot water pool, and the *sudatorium* (sweat room), if one was available. The aim was to gradually induce a cleansing perspiration. The bather then applied oil and scraped it off again, taking away any dirt and grime in the process. A brief return visit to the *frigidarium* closed the pores before the bather dressed and left.

Dedications to the goddess Fortuna are common in bathhouses, no doubt to protect the bathers in their naked state. A beautifully cut alter from Neckarburken (Germany), dated to AD 158, records how the garrison of the small fort proudly fulfilled their vow to Fortuna by 'restoring the bathhouse which had fallen down through old age, adding vaulted ceilings in tilework, and even putting new fittings in place' (*balineum vetustate conlabsum adiecta concha et camaris opere figlino restitutis item vasis novis positis*: AE 1986, 523). The female head of a statuette found in the Bearsden bathhouse is probably Fortuna, but other deities were remembered, too. The famous seven niches in the Chesters bathhouse are often explained as clothes lockers, but would have provided rather limited storage space while maximizing the potential for loss of property and pilfering. More probably, they held some religious significance, perhaps as the settings for statuettes.

Baths buildings were as prone to accidental damage as any others, and perhaps more so, given their reliance on furnaces to feed the hypocaust system and heat the water. An inscription from the aptly named fort of Lavatris (Bowes, England) explains, with admirable frankness, that the provincial governor 'restored the bathhouse which had been destroyed by violent fire' (*balineum vi ignis exustum … restituit*: RIB 730). A fragmentary inscription re-used in Cliburn Church, but perhaps originally from the fort at Brougham (England), seemingly alludes to a similar situation (following the restoration proposed by the epigrapher R. P. Wright): 'the bathhouse [was rebuilt] after the old work had been burnt and fallen into ruin' (*balineum […] veteri opere exusto in ruinam dilabsum*: RIB 791).

Elsewhere along the frontiers, bathhouses required the same care and maintenance as any other major building. The inscription set up by *cohors II Flavia Commagenorum* at the Dacian fort of Micia (Vetel, Romania), recording the repair of their dilapidated bathhouse by Septimius Severus

The *balneum* at Walldürn (Baden-Württemberg) on the outer *limes* of Upper Germany, dating from AD 232. This 'row type' bathhouse is similar to the one at Bearsden, with its timber-built changing room (right) giving access to a sequence of rooms. (© Dietwulf Baatz)

The turf-and-timber fort of Bothwellhaugh lies some 32km south of the Antonine Wall. Nothing is known of the interior, but a fine example of a *Reihentyp* ('row type') bathhouse was located 100m away, on lower ground near the river. It exhibits the standard progression of stone-built rooms, from the *frigidarium* (cold room) with plunge pool, through a pair of *tepidaria* (warm rooms), to the *caldarium* (hot room), which is nearest to the furnace. A timber-framed *apodyterium* (changing room) was added onto the side of the building. The local garrison will have striven to bring the bathhouse, like other military buildings, under the protection of a deity, usually the goddess Fortuna.

(*Imperator ... balneas cohortis ... vetustate dilabsas restituit*: CIL 3, 1374), is not unusual. Nor is the fact that the same bathhouse required further repair under Severus Alexander (AE 1903, 66). The fort had already been refurbished in stone under Antoninus Pius, 40 years earlier. A similar story can be told about the fort of Jagsthausen (Germany), where the dilapidated bathhouse was also repaired during the time of Septimius Severus (*balneum ... vetustate dilabsum a solo restitutum*: AE 1995, 1165). And the same bathhouse was repaired once again, 50 years later, when the emperor Philippus and his son 'restored the ruined bathhouse of the First Cohort of Germans' (*Imperatores ...balineum cohortis I Germanorum vetustate conlabsum restituerunt*: AE 1995, 1166). Of course, in each case, it was the soldiers who repaired the bathhouse, but with imperial blessing. And it is noteworthy that the tribune at Jagsthausen set up a separate dedication 'in honour of the sacred goddess Fortuna, restorer of the baths' (*In honorem deae Fortunae sanctae balineari reduci*: ILS 2605).

Dozens of inscriptions using a very similar formulation are known from forts throughout the empire. For example, in AD 232, the *numerus* in garrison at Walldürn (Germany) set up a dedication to Sacred Fortuna, reporting that 'they restored the bathhouse which had fallen down through old age' (*balineum vetustate conlapsum ... restituerunt*: ILS 9184 = AE 1983, 729); archaeology has revealed that the bathhouse was indeed remodelled and enlarged. Similarly, a tribune marked his time at Risingham (England) by making a dedication to Fortuna the Restorer 'on completion of the bathhouse' (*explicito balineo*: RIB 1212).

Communal latrine at Housesteads. The main sewer, visible as a deep channel running around the inside wall, would have been covered by wooden seating. The channel that can be seen in the floor carried water for the soldiers to rinse their sponges. (© Author)

Even the little Severan guard post of Thenadassa (Ain Wif, Libya) had a substantial bathhouse that evidently required repair at some point. An inscription from the site records that the commander 'supervised the repair of the bathhouse, which was ruined through old age, built a sweating room from scratch, and established a *cylisterium*' (*balneum vetustate corruptum restituendum curavit eidem assam cellam a solo fecit et cylisterium instituit*: AE 1950, 127). The precise nature of the *cylisterium*, clearly a building of some sort, is unknown (although a link with the Greek *xylon* seems possible, and may hint at a timber store, perhaps for the furnace).

An interesting variation is apparent at the fort of Lanchester (England). There, during the reign of Gordian III (AD 238–44), *cohors I Lingonum* gratefully recorded that the emperor 'built a bathhouse and exercise hall from the ground up' (*balineum cum basilica a solo instruxit*: RIB 1091 = ILS 2620). The same combination of buildings is mentioned around 25 years later at the fort of Lancaster, where the remains of a fine bathhouse were excavated in the 1970s. This time, the garrison, horsemen of *ala Sebussiana*, refurbished their baths and totally rebuilt the dilapidated exercise hall (*balineum refectum et basilicam vetustate conlabsum a solo restitutam*: RIB 605 = ILS 2548). These must have been palatial baths complexes; the big legionary *thermae* routinely had exercise halls built on (see Fortress 43, p. 46–47), but auxiliary bathhouses were usually more modest affairs.

The water supply

The water supply was an important part of any fort. On 4 December AD 241, during the reign of Gordian III, the prefect of *cohors I Septimia Belgarum* at Öhringen (Germany) erected an altar to the immortal Nymphs, announcing

The fort at Eining displays the classic playing-card shape. The foundations of the *principia* can be seen in the centre. In the 4th century AD, the defences were reduced to occupy only the south-west corner (top left). (© Dietwulf Baatz)

The 1.6ha fort of Tokod (Hungary) on the frontier of Pannonia Superior dates from the reign of Valentinian I (AD 364–75). The corner towers take the form of an elongated U shape, making it easier to enfilade the walls to either side. (© Sandra Walkshofer)

that 'he brought the Gordianic stream, which had long been neglected, through a new conduit 5,907 feet long [1.75km] into the *praetorium* and baths' (*aquam Gordianam … multo tempore intermissam … novo aquaeductu perduxit per pedes V milia DCCCCVII quam salere instituit in praetorium et in balineum*: CIL 13, 11759). The water supply had perhaps been neglected during the years of Alamannic warfare, but it was over 50 years since a centurion of *legio VIII Augusta* had 'brought water [into the fort] because there was none' (*quod aqua non esset induxit*: CIL 13, 11757). At Chester-le-Street (England), an inscription of AD 216 perhaps records the leading of an aqueduct across the fort's territory in order to bring water to the bathhouse, but the crucial part of the inscription has been lost (*[aquam per agros t]erritoriumque [… per pedes X] induxit [et balneum militum a s]olo in[struxit]*: RIB 1049, with suggestions from AE 1952, 12). Archaeology revealed such a ground-level aqueduct, almost ten kilometres long, serving the Hadrian's Wall fort of Great Chesters.

The latrines

Sanitation was very important to the Roman military. In many forts, an elaborate system of water tanks, gutters and drains can still be seen, for gathering and distributing rainwater. Communal latrines were normally built into this system of waste disposal, ideally positioned against the rampart at the lowest point on the site, to ensure that the sewage was promptly flushed away. Of course, the outfall from the fort inevitably ended up in the ditch, from which it perhaps required periodic removal.

At Bearsden, the fort ditch outside the latrine was found to contain sewage, which proved to be rich in food residue. In particular, cereal bran, fig seeds and the remains of blackberries, raspberries and hazel nuts were present, while traces of coriander, dill, linseed, mallow and poppy could have been used for medicinal purposes. The deposit also contained fragments of moss, which had perhaps been substituted for the sponges normally used in Roman toilets. No indication of meat eating was found, although evidence from other forts points to the consumption, at least occasionally, of beef, mutton, pork and chicken.

Late Roman fort at Qasr Bshir (Jordan), c. AD 300

In the late period, small fortifications like Qasr Bshir were still considered to be *castella*. But, being much smaller than even the 'small forts' of previous centuries, Qasr Bshir is perhaps best described as a *quadriburgium*. This late type of fort was characterized by its four massive corner towers, interior courtyard, and single, heavily defended entrance. Unusually, a building inscription survives *in situ* above the entrance, dedicating the fort's construction 'to our best and greatest rulers', Diocletian and his colleague Maximian, and 'the most noble Caesars', Constantius Chlorus and Galerius, the four members of the Tetrarchy.

AFTERMATH: AUXILIARY FORTS IN THE LATER PERIOD

By the later 3rd century AD, the more troubled conditions on the frontiers led to the development of more robust fort defences. We find the increasing prevalence of projecting towers to enable defensive enfilading techniques, the extension of ditch systems incorporating five or six lines, and the narrowing of gateways. All of these measures can be found as far back as the Severan dynasty, but their widespread adoption under the Tetrarchy, Diocletian's 'rule by four men', indicates a new defensive awareness in the later Roman Army. An undated inscription from Ambleside (England) referring to the death of a records clerk (*actarius*), 'killed inside the fort by the enemy' (*in castello interfectus ab hostibus*: AE 1964, 169) perhaps belongs to this later period.

At Eining in Raetia, the garrison of the 1.8ha fort, which dated back to Flavian times, had suffered from the 3rd-century attacks of the Alamanni on

In the late period, the fort of Favianis (Mautern, Austria) was reduced in area and received projecting towers. It was strategically placed on the frontier in Noricum to watch a major crossing of the Danube. (© Sandra Walkshofer)

Aerial view of the Flavian fort at Cardean, showing as a cropmark. From ground level, the fort is invisible, but differential crop growth above the ditches creates a pattern that can be seen from above. The outer ditch encloses an annexe (left). (© David Woolliscroft)

more than one occasion. *Cohors III Britannorum*, the same unit that had rebuilt the fort in stone under Hadrian, still dutifully manned their post 200 years later. But now, they withdrew into a tiny 0.16ha fortification, laid out in the south-west corner of the existing fort. Other fort garrisons enhanced their defences. At Remagen in Lower Germany, after a brief period of inactivity, *cohors I Flavia Hispanorum equitata* thickened the fort wall and added a circular projecting corner tower, ideal for enfilading the adjoining walls. And at Drobeta, the internal corner and interval towers were extended to project beyond the walls, and three of the four gates were closed and converted into bastions. The *porta praetoria* received rounded towers that projected six metres beyond the gateway, and the corner towers were extended in a fan shape.

Along the eastern frontier, forts were established with the same telltale projecting corner and interval towers. But they incorporated the local peculiarity of locating buildings against the outer wall, occupying the usual

Reconstructed north gate at Weißenburg (Germany). This was the fort's rear gate (*porta decumana*). It was remodelled, prior to the abandonment of the outer *limes* in AD 260, with semicircular projecting towers. (© Dietwulf Baatz)

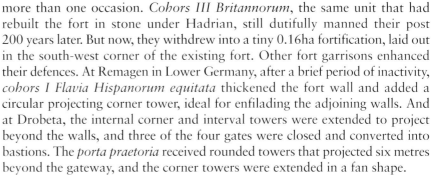

intervallum space. At Da'ajaniya (Jordan), the square one-hectare fort has 2.25m thick walls; observers in the later 19th century claimed that the wall-walk stood at a height of 4.7m. Similarly, at the little 0.3ha fort of Qasr Bshir (Jordan), the three-storey projecting corner towers still stand to about ten metres. Each fort is served by a single entrance, and departs from the earlier standard layout of a centrally placed *principia* at the junction of the two main roads. In fact, Qasr Bshir is little more than a courtyard surrounded by ranges of two-storey rooms, built against the outer walls. A famous inscription on the lintel above the gate proclaims its Tetrarchic date (CIL 3, 14149) and gives the fort's name (as re-read by Kennedy) as Castra Praetorium Mobene.

The 2.7ha fort at Pfünz (Bayern) was excavated in the late 19th century. It is not known whether it survived the Alamannic depredations of AD 233. The north wall from the main gate (*porta praetoria*) to the north-west corner tower has been reconstructed for visitors. (© Dietwulf Baatz)

Sixty years on, the military historian Ammianus Marcellinus, writing about contemporary events, records how Valentinian I (AD 364–75) placed a high priority on refortifying the frontiers, after years of neglect. On one occasion, his hasty approach led him to site a fort badly, where its foundations were in danger of being undermined by a river; but his solution was to set his men the onerous task of diverting the stream (Amm. Marc. 28.2.2–4). Valentinian's last act was to receive a Germanic embassy, who complained about the building of a Roman fort on their territory across the Danube, at which the emperor flew into so furious a rage that he took an apoplectic fit and died (Amm. Marc. 30.6.1–6).

The 1.6ha Valentinianic fort at Tokod (Hungary) is typical of late Roman forts, with its single gate and projecting corner and interval towers. A small garrison, less inclined to fight in the open, had no need for multiple gates, which simply represented multiple weak points to be defended. Equally, a defensive garrison valued the provision of strong projecting towers, from which to dominate an enemy clustering outside the walls. Forts like Tokod characterized a different Roman mindset from that of Augustus and Trajan, and a different Roman Army.

THE SITES TODAY

Most Roman forts have left no traces above ground. Some have been identified through the techniques of aerial reconnaissance, whereby ancient disturbance of the landscape, long ago ploughed flat, occasionally reveals itself by discoloration or differential growth in crops, a phenomenon only really observable from above. Other sites survive as flattened platforms and faintly detectable ditch systems, again best viewed from a high vantage point. Archaeologists have investigated many of these, so that, where the evidence has not been entirely obliterated by later activity, we have some idea of what once existed on the site.

Only rarely is a site so well preserved that the visitor can readily discern the ancient remains and envisage the fort in its heyday. Some of the best examples are along Hadrian's Wall, at the well-known sites of Housesteads, Chesters (Northumberland) and Wallsend (Tyne & Wear). At many other sites, key features have been consolidated for visitors, or even reconstructed to assist our interpretation. Some of the best examples of this lie along the Upper German and Raetian frontier (the so-called ORL, 'Obergermanische–Raetischer Limes'), where they are often combined with an excellent museum, as at Saalburg (Bad Homburg v.d.H., Hessen) and Aalen (Baden-Württemberg). Full-size fort gateways have even been built, for example, at South Shields (Tyne & Wear), and at Weißenburg and Pfünz (Bayern). As the 'Frontiers of the Roman Empire' World Heritage Site gradually gathers momentum, we can surely look forward to more examples of forts laid out for the general public.

FURTHER READING

The few English-language books that describe auxiliary forts have concentrated on examples from Britain, while German publications have concentrated on the sites of the Rhine frontier, in present-day Germany and the Netherlands. The forts along the Danube frontier are less well known in the English-speaking world, because their excavations are reported in the national journals of Austria, Hungary, Bulgaria and Romania, which are less accessible to researchers in the UK. The most up-to-date English-language information on these can be found in John Wilkes's 2005 survey. Coverage of other frontiers is patchy, with the exception of Jordan, recently summarized by David Kennedy.

On the auxiliary units themselves, the classic work is Leonard Cheesman's 1914 monograph, to be read in conjunction with Denis Saddington's more up-to-date (but chronologically limited) treatment. Almost every year brings more scholarly articles discussing various aspects of the auxiliary forces. Perhaps most important of these, in recent years, has been Paul Holder's survey of auxiliary deployment under Hadrian. And on the daily routine of the men who manned the forts, the volume of papers by the late Roy Davies has much of interest. (See bibliography for all of these.)

Select bibliography

Baatz, D., *Der römische Limes* (4th edn., Berlin: Gebr. Mann, 2000)

Bailey, G. B., 'The provision of fort-annexes on the Antonine Wall', *Proceedings of the Society of Antiquaries of Scotland* 124 (1994), 299–314

Bennett, J., 'Fort sizes as a guide to garrison type', C. Unz (ed.), *Studien zu den Militärgrenzen Roms III* (Stuttgart: Theiss, 1986), 707–16

Cheesman, G. L., *The Auxilia of the Roman Imperial Army* (Oxford: Clarendon Press, 1914; repr. Chicago: Ares Publishers, 1975)

Davies, R. (eds. D. Breeze & V. Maxfield), *Service in the Roman Army* (Edinburgh: Edinburgh University Press, 1989)

Glasbergen, W., & Groenman-van Waateringe, W., *The Pre-Flavian Garrisons of Valkenburg z.H.* (Amsterdam: North Holland Publishing Co., 1974)

Hassall, M., 'The Internal Planning of Roman Auxiliary Forts', B. Hartley and J. Wacher (eds.), *Rome and her Northern Provinces* (Gloucester: Alan Sutton,1983), 96–131

Hodgson, N., & Bidwell, P., 'Auxiliary Barracks in a New Light: Recent Discoveries on Hadrian's Wall', *Britannia* 35 (2004), 121–57

Holder, P. A., 'Auxiliary Deployment in the Reign of Hadrian', in: J. J. Wilkes (ed.), *Documenting the Roman Army* (London: Institute of Classical Studies, 2003), 101–45

Johnson, A. (ed. D. Baatz), *Römische Kastelle* (Mainz: Philipp von Zabern, 1987)

Kennedy, D. L., *The Roman Army in Jordan* (London: Council for British Research in the Levant, 2000)

Saddington, D. B., *The Development of the Roman Auxiliary Forces from Caesar to Vespasian* (Harare, 1982)

Wilkes, J. J., 'The Roman Danube: an archaeological survey', *Journal of Roman Studies* 95 (2005), 124–225

GLOSSARY

Aedes (principiorum) shrine and repository of the standards, situated centrally at the rear of the *principia* (*q.v.*)

Ala cavalry unit (pl. *alae*), nominally 500 strong (*ala quingenaria*) or 1,000 strong (*ala milliaria*)

Ballistarium store building for the arrow-shooting catapults (*ballistae*) of the 2nd to 4th centuries AD (attested only at High Rochester)

Balneum bathhouse, usually situated outside the ramparts of the fort (sometimes found as *balineum* in inscriptions)

Basilica equestris exercitatoria cavalry drill hall (attested only at Netherby)

Basilica (principiorum) collonaded hall comprising central nave and side aisles, situated across the width of the *principia*, either between the courtyard and the rear suite of rooms, or (less commonly) spanning the *via principalis* in front of the *principia* (*q.v.*)

Centuria subdivision of an infantry cohort (pl. *centuriae*), probably numbering 80 men

Centurio centurion (pl. *centuriones*), commander of an infantry *centuria* (*q.v.*)

Contubernium squad of men (pl. *contubernia*), thought to occupy a double barrack room

Decurio decurion (pl. *decuriones*), commander of a cavalry *turma* (*q.v.*)

Fabrica manufacturing workshop (pl. *fabricae*)

Horreum granary building (pl. *horrea*), designed to store grain and other foodstuffs

Intervallum free space between the rampart and the buildings in the fort, occupied by the *via sagularis* (*q.v.*)

Latera praetorii the central range of buildings within the fort (lit. 'flanks of the *praetorium*'), fronting onto the *via principalis*

Porta decumana rear gate of the fort

Porta praetoria main gate of the fort

Porta principalis side gate of the fort (pl. *portae principales*), designated *sinistra* (left) or *dextra* (right) depending upon its position relative to the *principia* (*q.v.*)

Praetentura the forward area within the fort, extending from the main gate (*porta praetoria*) to the main lateral roadway (*via principalis*), and normally filled with barrack blocks

Praetorium the commander's residence, normally in the central range of the fort

Principia the headquarters building, centrally located in the fort and incorporating administrative offices and the *aedes* (*q.v.*)

Retentura the rear area within the fort, extending from the rear gate (*porta decumana*) up to the secondary lateral roadway (*via quintana*), and normally filled with barrack blocks

Tabularium office (pl. *tabularia*), several of which were arranged along the rear of the *principia* (*q.v.*)

Turma subdivision of a cavalry *ala* (pl. *turmae*), thought to number 30 or 32 troopers

Tribunal raised platform for a commanding officer to address the troops

Valetudinarium hospital

Via decumana secondary longitudinal roadway in the fort, running from the rear gate (*porta decumana*) through the *retentura*, up to the *via quintana*

Via praetoria main longitudinal roadway in the fort, running from the front gate (*porta praetoria*) through the *praetentura*, up to the door of the *principia* (*q.v.*)

Via principalis main lateral roadway through a fort, running across the front of the *principia* and linking the two *portae principales*

Via sagularis perimeter roadway, running around the *intervallum* (*q.v.*)

INDEX OF FORTS

Figures in **bold** refer to illustrations.